Franz Lehár

THE MERRY WIDOW

Complete Score for Piano and Voice in English

Adapted from the German of Victor Léon and Leo Stein
Lyrics by Adrian Ross
Arranged for the Piano by H. M. Riggs

Dover Publications, Inc., New York

Published in Canada by General Publishing Company, Ltd., 30 Lesmill Road, Don Mills, Toronto, Ontario.
Published in the United Kingdom by Constable and Company, Ltd., 10 Orange Street, London WC2H 7EG.

This Dover edition, first published in 1983, is an unabridged republication of the work as published by Chappell & Co., London, in 1907.

Manufactured in the United States of America
Dover Publications, Inc., 180 Varick Street, New York, N.Y. 10014

Library of Congress Cataloging in Publication Data

Lehár, Franz, 1870–1948.
[Lustige Witwe. Vocal score. English]
The merry widow.

Operetta.
Libretto by Victor Léon and Leo Stein.
Based on: L'attaché d'ambassade / Henri Meilhac.
Reprint. Originally published: London: Chappell, 1907.
1. Operas—Vocal scores with piano. I. Léon, Victor, 1860–1940. II. Stein, Leo, 1862–1920. III. Meilhac, Henri, 1831–1897. Attaché d'ambassade. IV. Title.
M1503.L518L82 1983 83-5151
ISBN 0-486-24514-4

Dramatis Personae

BARON POPOFF *(Marsovian Ambassador)*
NATALIE *(his Wife)*
PRINCE DANILO *(Embassy Attaché)*
SONIA GLAWARD *(A Young Widow)*
VICOMTE CAMILLE DE JOLIDON
MARQUIS DE CASCADA
M. RAOUL DE ST. BRIOCHE
M. KHADJA *(Of the Embassy)*
MALITZA *(his Wife)*
GENERAL NOVA KOVICH *(Of the Embassy)*
OLGA *(his Wife)*
NISCH *(Messenger of Embassy)*

PRASKOVIA
AN ENGLISHMAN

FIFI
LOLO
DODO
JOU-JOU
FROU-FROU
CLO-CLO
MARGOT
ZO-ZO
SAPHO
(Girls at Maxim's)

Synopsis of Scenery

ACT I. The Marsovian Embassy, in Paris.
ACT II. Grounds of Sonia's House near Paris.
ACT III. Maxim's Restaurant, Paris.

Contents

ACT I.

ACT II.

ACT III.

Franz Lehár

THE MERRY WIDOW

Complete Score for Piano and Voice in English

THE MERRY WIDOW.

No. 1. Act I.

OPENING CHORUS.

Words by
ADRIAN ROSS.

Music by
FRANZ LEHAR.
Arranged for the Piano by H. M. HIGGS.

Marcia.

Allegretto.
St B.
la - dies and gen - tle - men real - ly I think that the du - ty's mine, To
p
5
speak our thanks to our host - ess, But speak - ing is not in my line. And so I'll
fz
mf
rit:
try but ve - ry brief - ly. To ex - press what I want to chief - ly; To the
Moderato.
charm - ing Bar - on - ess Pop - off, Join in a heart - y toast with

St B.
me!
NATALIE
I
Three times three to Bar_on_ess__ Pop_off, Hail her a_gain with three times three!
CHO.
Three times three to Bar_on_ess__ Pop_off. Hail her a_gain with three times three!
Three times three to Baron_ess Pop_off. Hail her a_gain with three times three!
mf
Allegro.
NAT.
thank you dou_bly for your kind_ness That you so heart_i_ly ex_
p
rit:
allargando
NAT.
_press, It makes me proud both as your host_ess And as a
rit:
3

NAT.
animato
true Am - bas - sa - dress. This par - ty has a dou - ble
mf
p
NAT.
mean - ing, For when your plea - sure you e - vince You hon - our our sove - reign, His
rit.
p
NAT.
Tempo di Mazurka.
High - ness, Mar - so - via's great and no - ble Prince. Your
p
NAT.
kind ex - pres - sions will con - tent him, For when I bid you come to
mf
NAT.
dance Un wor - thi - ly I rep - re - sent him; I'm Mar - so - via, here in
p
f

NATALIE.
France Your kind ex_pres_sions will con_tent him, For when I bid you come to dance Un_
SYLVAINE.
We hope it will not dis_con_tent him, If we should bless the lucky chance That
PRASKOVIA.
We hope it will not dis_con_tent him, If we should bless the lucky chance That
OLGA.
We hope it will not dis_con_tent him, If we should bless the lucky chance That
CAMILLE.
We hope it will not dis_con_tent him, If we should bless the lucky chance That
KHADJA.
We hope it will not dis_con_tent him, If we should bless the lucky chance That
St BRIOCHE.
We hope it will not dis_con_tent him, If we should bless the lucky chance That
CASCADA.
We hope it will not dis_con_tent him, If we should bless the lucky chance That
NOVIKOVICH.
We hope it will not dis_con_tent him, If we should bless the lucky chance That
CHO.
We hope it will not dis_con_tent him, If we should bless the lucky chance That
We hope it will not dis_con_tent him, If we should bless the lucky chance That
We hope it will not dis_con_tent him, If we should bless the lucky chance That

rit.

NAT. wor_thi_ly I rep_re_sent him, I'm Mar_so - via here in France.

SYL. sends you now to rep_re_sent him, As Mar_so - via here in France.

PRAS. sends you now to rep_re_sent him, As Mar_so - via here in France.

OLGA. sends you now to rep_re_sent him, As Mar_so - via here in France.

CAM. sends you now to rep_re_sent him, As Mar_so - via here in France.

KHAD. sends you now to rep_re_sent him, As M r_so - via here in France

St B. sends you now to rep_re_sent him, As Mar_so - via here in France.

CAS. sends you now to rep_re_sent him, As Mar_so - via here in France.

NOV. sends you now to rep_re_sent him, As Mar_so - via here in France.

CHO. sends you now to rep_re_sent him, As Mar_so - via here in France.
sends you now to rep_re_sent him, As Mar_so - via here in France.
sends you now to rep_re_sent him, As Mar_so - via here in France.

p rit. f 14

Allegro moderato.

ff fz

No. 1a

BALL-MUSIC.

No. 2.

DUET.– (Natalie and Camille.)

"A DUTIFUL WIFE."

CAM.
NATALIE.
that I must tell you too!
No, please!
I
tr
p
NAT.
rit.
CAMILLE.
a tempo
can - not lis - ten to words like these!
Yet you can hear them, tho' I am still,— I
rit.
pp a tempo
NATALIE.
That, dear - est friend, is what I have dread - ed.
CAM.
long to say them, and I will,— I will!
pp
NAT.
It's time this was end - ed—
It's time you were wed - ded!
CAM.
Was end - ed?
A wife for me?
f

Allegretto.

CAM.

That can-not be; For you are my love, the love ___ for me!

rit:

p *mf* *rit:*

a tempo

NAT.

I beg of you, dear, You will not tell me what I must not hear! For

pp a tempo

Allegretto moderato.

NAT.

I am a du-ti-ful wife, An-oth-er is lord of my life. It brings but trou-ble and dan-ger To lis-ten to love from a strang-er. My

pp *f* *p*

Ped. * Ped. * Ped. * Ped. * Ped. *

NAT.
vows I can nev - er re - call, So what is the end of it
all, But sor - row and per - il and strife, When I am a du - ti - ful
rit:
pp
p
Ped.
wife? I lose if I love — you, and what are you win - ning? Ah, break off this
a tempo
mf a tempo
dim:
Ped.
fol - ly while yet it's be - gin - ning! Take care, take care! my
rit:
Allegretto.
pp

NAT.
friend, be-ware! And do not play With fire to - day! Stamp
mf
pp
NAT.
out the brand Ere it is fanned, Or from its sleep The flame may
NAT.
leap! Tho' it may be but a child - ish game, Yet you may
p
NAT.
set your house a - flame! The blaze you start May sear your
mf
p

NAT.
heart! Play not with fire then, friend Be - ware!
CAM.
Allegretto moderato.
Yes, you are a du - ti - ful
mf
pp
wife; It goes to my heart like a knife! But spite of the bars that may
sev - - er, I love you, and love you for ev - - er! And
f
p
tho' we are al - ways a - part, The love will live on in my heart Un -
p

CAM.
-til I grow old in the strife, While you are- a du - ti - ful
pp
rit:
CAM.
wife! I know there is per - il, but yet I would dare— it! To lose you for
a tempo
mf
dim:
p
NATALIE. Allegretto.
Take care, take care! My
CAM.
ev - er, ah! how could I bear— it! I
Allegretto.
rit:
pp
NAT.
friend, be - ware! And do not play With fire to - day! Stamp
CAM.
mean to dare— I mean to dare, Though du - ty bars the way;
pp

NAT.
out the brand Ere it is fanned, Or from its sleep The flame may
CAM.
But du - ty's call, that is not all— Love
NAT.
leap! Though it may be but a child - ish game, Yet you may
CAM.
has a word to say. You will love me yet,
mf
p
NAT.
set your house a - flame! The blaze you start May sear your
CAM.
Take care, Be - ware, And in your heart The flame will start!
mf
p
NAT.
heart! Play not with fire, then, friend, Take care!
CAM.
For love will bid you dare, And then you will not care!
f
Ped. * Ped. * Ped. * Ped. *

No. 3. ENTRANCE. SONG.–(Sonia.) and CHORUS.

"IN MARSOVIA."

dim:

Tempo di Mazurka.

SONIA.

Gen-tle-men, I pray! How po-lite you are!

CASCADA.

We can-not tear our-selves a-way! From our ev'ning

p

SON.

What things you say! Stop it, pray! No more now, kind-ly,

St BRIOCHE.

We're daz-zled by your beau-ty's ray, Grop-ing blind-ly!

CAS.

star!

Ped. * Ped. *

SON.
St. B.
CAS.
CHO.
Gen - tle - men!
Now, don't re - peat it, pray!
Our heart - felt hom - age let us pay!
Be - fore our rul - ing
MALE CHORUS.
p
Ped.
rit:
You real - ly are too good to me, you are!
I have - n't been in
star, Our fair - - est star!

Mazurka.
SON.
Pa-ris long, And when I meet a man I'm al-ways say-ing
pp a tempo
something wrong, I'm so Mar-so-vi - an! For when a man would
Ped.
wed a girl In my own na-tive land, He does-n't call her
mf
p
star and pearl And want to kiss her hand. Says he, "Let
pp

Animato.
SON.
us get mar-ried now, We are both grow-ing big, My fa-ther has a cow, And your
Animato.
mf
cres:
mo - ther has a pig."
rit:
That's how it's done, you know, For
St BRIOCHE.
Oh!
CASCADA.
Oh!
CHO.
Oh!
Oh!
f rit:
f a tempo
rit:
p

Valse.
SON.
that is how we wed. There's no_thing more that need be said,
SON.
But ask Pa_pa and dear Mam_ma, That's how we mar_ry in Mar_so_vi_
SON.
_a! Ah!
St BRIOCHE.
Court_ing such as that Is ex_treme_ly
CASCADA.
Court_ing such as that Is ex_treme_ly
CHO.
Ha! ha! That's how they go!
Ha! ha! That's how they go!
mf
mf

SON.
St B.
CAS.
CHO.
Look out for mon - ey, then ask Pa-
flat! We don't do it so!
flat! We don't do it so!
We do it so really you know!
We do it so really you know!
rit:
pa When you're in Mar - so - vi - a!
Allegro.
St BRIOCHE.
When you are
CASCADA.
When you are
Tell us some more of your
Tell us some more of your
Allegro.
f a tempo

SON.
St. B.
CAS.
CHO.
SONIA:
rit.
With us a marriage
mar - ried Tell us what then?
mar - ried Tell us what then?
wo - men and men! When they are mar - ried, Well, what then?
wo - men and men! When they are mar - ried, Well, what then?
rit.
rit.
Mazurka.
is for life. We don't ad-mire di - vorce. If some-one courts an-
Real - - ly? Tru - - ly?
Real - - ly? Tru - - ly?
Real - - ly? Tru - - ly?
Real - - ly? Tru - - ly?
pp

SON.
-oth-er's wife, He will be shot, of course. And if a wife to
St. B.
If a wife is un - ru - - ly?
CAS.
If a wife is un - ru - - ly?
CHO
If a wife is un - ru - - ly?
If a wife is un - ru - - ly?
SON.
oth - er men Should give a look or two, Her hus-band takes a
St. B.
Then her hus - - band.—
CAS.
Then her hus - - band.—
CHO.
Then her hus - - band.—
Then her hus - - band.—
mf
p

SON.
cud_gel then. And beats her black and blue! Men are all the same, I
St B.
Thrash_es her black and blue!
CAS.
Thrash_es her black and blue!
CHO.
Thrash_es her black and blue! Oh
Thrash_es her black and blue! Oh
pp
p
Ped.
Ped.
SON.
can see! You could beat your wives, I fan_cy!
St B.
If you mar_ried me,— On_ly try and
CAS.
If you mar_ried me,— On_ly try and
CHO.
no! Ma_dame, oh no!
no! Ma_dame, oh no!

SON.
Ha, ha, ha, ha, ha! Just as in Mar-so-vi-
St. B.
see! Ah, I don't do so!
CAS.
see! Ah, I don't do so!
CHO.
Real-ly, you know! That is not so!
Real-ly, you know! That is no so!
mf
SON.
-a, As we do in
rit:
St. B.
A wo-man I would nev-er strike!
rit:
CAS.
CHO.
p rit:

SON.
St B.
CAS.
CHO.
Mar - so - vi - a!
Ha!
We're not in Mar - so - vi -
I'll let you beat me if you like.
Allegro.
ha!
- a!
Allegro

No. 3a. BALL-MUSIC.

Nº 4. SONG.–(Danilo.)

"MAXIM'S."

DAN.
working so exhausts a man, And I take all the rest I
can; I need a sleep to put me right, And that's why
I sit up all night! I'm very busy at my club: We have a
hundred on the rub; I lose a thousand of the best, Then
pp
mf
tr
fz
mf
f

DAN.
get the girls to take the rest. I go off to Max - im's, Where
p rit.
p a tempo
AN.
fun and fro - lic beams, With all the girls I chat - ter, I
DAN.
laugh and kiss and flat - ter! Lo - lo, Do - do, Jou - jou, Clo -
p
DAN.
- clo, Mar - got, Frou - frou! For sur - names do not mat - ter. I take the first to
f

Animato.
DAN.
hand And, then the corks go pop, We dance and nev - er
pp
stop, The La - dies smile so sweet - ly, I catch and kiss them
neat - ly! Lo - lo, Do - do, Jou - jou, Clo - clo, Mar - got, Frou -
p
- frou. Till I for - get com - plete - ly My dear old Fa - ther
f

Allegretto moderato.
DAN.
-im's 2. Then I re-fresh my ja-ded brain With lit-tle
sup-pers and cham-pagne. And look in-to the la-dies'
eyes Till they and I are close al-lies! So
in a glass of gold-en wine. An en-tente
pp
mf
tr
Ped.

DAN.
cor - di - ale I sign; For I can do that sort of
mf
DAN.
thing, As well as an - y oth - er king! Then
fz
DAN.
I al_low the love_ly sex To wear my arms a_round their necks, And
mf
DAN.
give the wai_ter at the door An or_der for a doz_en more! I'm
f
p rit:
p

DAN.
hap - py at Max - im's, Where fun and fro - lic beams! With
a tempo
all the girls I chat - ter, I laugh and kiss and flat - ter! Lo -
p
- lo, Do - do, Jou - jou, Clo - clo, Mar - got, Frou - frou, For
Ped. *
Animato.
sur - names do not mat - ter I take the first to hand And, then the corks go
8
pp

DAN.
pop, We dance and nev - er stop The la - dies smile so sweet - ly, I
8
catch and kiss them neat - ly Lo - lo, Do - do, Jou - jou, Clo -
p
Ped.
- clo, Mar - got, Frou - frou Till I for - get com - plete - ly My dear old Fa - ther-
f
-land.
Allegro.
f
ff
fz

Nº 5. SONG. (Camille.)

"HOME."

CAM.
To wan - der through that ma - gic land. That is the
pp
ma - gic that fills the hap - py home, The storm - y
world may be wild as o - cean foam, We shall not
care what the wea - ry world may do, You're all the
world to me, and I to you.

Più lento.
CAM.
Ah, that is all to live for tru - ly, Can hap - pi - ness be
p
found else - where? On - ly the sun and sky a - bove
Smil - ing on me and her I love!
Ah, when the world is
all un - ru - ly, One re - fuge we can find from care,
It is the home, It is our home and hap - pi - ness is there, yes there.
rit:
fz

Allegretto.
CAM.
p
mf
pp
Yet all the love-ly dream Is but a bub-ble's gleam,
A rain-bow's mag-ic ray That breaks and fades a-way,
The home I thought so fair We find not a-ny-where,
'Tis but a cas-tle in the air. That is the

CAM.
vis - ion of hap - pi - ness at home,
But in the
CAM.
search for it vain - ly we may roam.
The world is
CAM.
cold that we have to wan - der through,
Though you're the
CAM.
world to me and I to you.
p

CAM.
Ped.
You're all my world, I'm the world to
you.
Allegro.
mf animato
p
pp
rit.
f
8

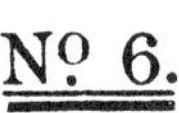

FINALE.—ACT I.

BALL-MUSIC.

Tempo di Valse.

Piano.

mf

Tempo di Marcia.

MALE CHORUS.

CHO.

La_dies' choice! That's the u - ni - ver_sal voice! So, Madame, may I demand The

La_dies' choice! That's the u - ni - ver_sal voice! So, Madame, may I demand The

Tempo di Marcia.

mf

CHO.

high_est hon_our of your hand? One dance-just one a_lone To call my ve_ry own!

high_est hon_our of your hand? One dance-just one a_lone To call my ve_ry own!

fz

fz

CHO.
Su-preme-ly hap-py I should be If you had cho - sen me!
Su-preme-ly hap-py I should be If you had cho - sen me!
mf
SONIA.
Gen-tle-men, Tho' of course I like to dance with an - y, What am I to
p
fz
SON.
say to ten? I can-not take so ma - ny. I had best sit
fz
p
SON.
out the dance, Give the o-ther girls a chance. There are partners here in
p
fz

SON.
plenty!
St.BRIOCHE.
(aside)
più animato
Not with millions, sweet and twen_ty! They're get_ting ve_ry pressing now, I must
MALE CHORUS.
CHO.
Just a dance! On_ly one! Just a sin_gle dance!
Just a dance! On_ly one! Just a sin_gle dance!
f
ff
f
fz
più animato
St.B.
put them off some_how- Yes, I'll put them off some_how.
Allegro.
fz
f
St.B.
Più lento.
They're like flies a_round the hon_ey,
Più lento.
p

Tempo di Marcia moderato.
St. B.
They shall not get the widow's mon - ey.
CASCADA.
I
fz p
CAS
say, don't you know this is wrong of you, It's con_duct that grieves us and pains. If
pp
ST. BRIOCHE.
You
CAS
you do not dance, what are we to do But go off and blow out our brains?
fz
f pp
ST. B.
wo_men go in for the vote, they say, And want to be e_qual with man; And

ST. B.
now that to-night is e - lec - tion day, You won't give a vote when you can!
CASCADA.
Then pray re -
fz
mf
f
ST. B.
Then do not spurn me! E - lec - tor! May I ask your vote and
CAS.
- turn me! E - lec - tor! May I ask your vote and
ST. B.
voice? Give your vote to Saint Brio - che! I am the
CAS.
voice? Mind and plump for Cas - ca - da! I am the
fz
fz
p

ST. B.
CAS.
CHO.
par_ty de_serv_ing your choice!
Give your vote to
par_ty de_serv_ing your choice!
Mind and plump for Cas_ca_da!
MALE CHORUS.
Don't you vote for
Don't you plump for Cas_ca_da!
f
fz
SONIA.
I'm
Saint Brio_che!
I am the par_ty de_serv_ing your choice!
I am the par_ty de_serv_ing your choice!
Saint Brio_che!
I am the par_ty de_serv_ing your choice!
I am the par_ty de_serv_ing your choice!
fz
f
f
pp

SON.
not a po-lit-i-cal la-dy, I hate giv-ing votes, and all
SON.
that! It makes a man do what is sha-dy, And
fz
SON.
ru-ins a wo-man's best hat! But now as you're all of you
f
pp
SON.
stand-ing, And say that you won't leave me still, I'll

SON.
do what you all are de - mand - ing: You ask me to vote - and I
fz
SON.
will!
I have to think be-fore I give my
ST. BRIOCHE.
Then do not spurn me!
CASCADA.
Then pray re-turn me!
8
mf
f
SON.
voice! Now in what di - rec - tion Shall I make se - lec - tion? Who is the
8
fz
fz
p

SON.
party de-serv-ing my choice? Now, in what di-rec-tion Shall I make se-
ST. BRIOCHE.
Look in my di-
CASCADA.
I'm up for e-lec-tion!
MALE CHORUS.
CHO.
Look in my di-
I'm up for e-lec-tion!
SON.
-lec-tion? Who is the par-ty de-serv-ing my choice?
ST. B.
-rec-tion! I am the par-ty de-serv-ing your choice!
CAS.
I am the par-ty de-serv-ing your choice!
CHO.
-rec-tion! I am the par-ty de-serv-ing your choice!
I am the par-ty de-serv-ing your choice!

Allegretto.
SONIA.
Well, then, gen_tle _ men,
You have been nom_in _ a _ ted for e _
pp
Ped.
SON.
_ lec _ tion:
Then I'll vote _ The die is
fz
SON.
animato
cast!
DANILO. (brings in LADIES)
Help has come to me at last!
LADIES. (off)
Ladies' choice! La_dies' choice!
f animato
ff
fz
Tempo di Valse. rit.
a tempo
DAN.
Oh, come a _ way, a _ way! Mu - sic is call - ing, With its
p rit.
a tempo

DAN.
magic charm enthralling! To its ringing and singing You
mf
pp
DAN.
lift your feet, Follow the chime of the time Of the waltz's beat!
mf
p
mf
rit.
a tempo
DAN.
Oh, come away, away! Music is playing, Linger not, vain-
rit
mf a tempo
fz
DAN.
ly delaying, Take your partners, choice is free!

1 LADY (to a MAN)
(both dance off)
Will you please, Sir, dance with me?
ff
SONIA.
For the
pp
SON.
night of the ball will go by,
And the dawn will be cold in the
SON.
sky.
Let us cap - ture our joys as they fly,
mf

SON.
Soon will they fade and die! There's a charm in the
fz
p
SON.
thrill of the strings, Like the beat of the Doves with their wings
rit.
SON.
Then a - way! No de - lay! Let us dance while we may, For our pleas - ure will
rit.
a tempo
SON.
end with day!
LADIES.
Take your part - ners don't de - lay!
f a tempo

SONIA.
Oh, come a - way, a - way! Mus - ic is call - ing, With its

DANILO.
Oh, come a - way, a - way! Mus - ic is call - ing, With its

ST. BRIOCHE.
Oh, come a - way, a - way! Mus - ic is call - ing, With its

CASCADA.
Oh, come a - way, a - way! Mus - ic is call - ing, With its

CHO.
Oh, come a - way, a - way!. Mus - ic is call - ing, With its
Oh, come a - way, a - way! Mus - ic is call - ing, With its

f

SON.
mag - ic charm en - thrall - ing! To its ring - ing and sing - ing You

DAN.
mag - ic charm en - thrall - ing! To its ring - ing and sing - ing You

ST. B.
mag - ic charm en - thrall - ing! To its ring - ing and sing - ing You

CAS.
mag - ic charm en - thrall - ing! To its ring - ing and sing - ing You

CHO.
mag - ic charm en - thrall - ing! To its ring - ing and sing - ing You
mag - ic charm en - thrall - ing! To its ring - ing and sing - ing You

SON.
DAN.
ST. B.
CAS.
CHO.
lift your feet, Fol-low the chime of the time of the waltz-'s beat. Oh, come a-way, a-
way! Mus-ic is play-ing Don't you hear what it is
ff

SON.
DAN.
ST. B.
CAS.
CHO.
say - ing? To the dance, make no de - lay - ing!
Ped.
Till the night shall be gone Our dance goes on.
(aside)
Not

DAN.
one of them must have her hand, For
that would grieve my Fa - ther - land. I mean to
make the game too hot For flies a - round the honey - pot!
Picc.
cresc.
CASCADA. (to SONIA.)
Ma - dame, you have not spo - ken!
ST. BRIOCHE.
Give

ST. B.
SONIA.
me a word as tok - en! Yes, now the time has
SON.
DANILO. (aside)
come to choose. I'll have to try some cle - ver
cresc.
dimin.
DAN.
SONIA.
ruse. Dear me! what shall I an - swer?
pp
NATALIE. (with CAMILLE.)
May I pre - sent you a dan - cer?
DANILO.
Oh, con - found! An -
Ob.
Horn.
p
mf

NAT.
You
DAN.
-oth - er hang-ing round!
Marcia moderato.
NAT.
see him dance the pol-ka, I've tried him_ and I know; He
NAT.
al - so knows the ma - zur - ka, I've tried him, and it's_
NAT.
so. He's ev - en stu - died the cake walk I've

NAT.
tried him long a - go! And as a part - ner in a waltz, He's
fz
NAT.
sim - ply with-out an - y faults. So pray re - turn him, And do not
8
mf
NAT.
spurn him! But kind-ly let him have your vote and voice! Won't you plump for
p
NAT.
Jo - li - don! Give your vote to Jo - li - don! He is the part - ner des-erv - ing your
fz
fz

SONIA.
An-oth-er
NAT.
choice!
He is the
ST. BRIOCHE.
Give your vote to Saint Brio-che!
I am the
CASCADA.
Won't you plump for Cas-ca-da?
I am the
Don't you vote for Jo-li-don!
I am the
MEN.
Don't you vote for Jo-li-don!
I am the
f
Allegro.
SON.
can-di-date wait-ing my choice!
NAT.
par-ty de-serv-ing your choice!
CAMILLE.
Pray say, Ma-dame, your choice I
ST. B.
par-ty de-serv-ing your choice!
CAS.
par-ty de-serv-ing your choice!
MEN.
par-ty de-serv-ing your choice!
par-ty de-serv-ing your choice!
Allegro.
fz
mf
8va.

(sees DANILO.)
SON.
I rather think— maybe—
CAM.
am!
mf
f
rit.
If I must give my answer,
(aside.)
rit.
My chosen partner will be
mf
rit.
he Who doesn't seem to notice me!
a tempo
mf
fz
(to DANILO.)
Will you be my dancer?
DANILO.
rit.
I? No, Madame, I do not
fz
rit.

Allegretto moderato.
DAN.
SONIA.
dance!
In fact, you don't care for the
pp
SON.
DANILO.
chance?
Don't care? Oh, no! My dance, you told me
p
SONIA.
I did! What then?
DAN.
so!
The dance is mine then. gen - tle-
DAN.
- men, I can do what I like with it, As I think

SONIA.
Of course!
NATALIA.
What does he mean?
CAMILLE.
What does he mean?
DAN.
fit! That's so? This dance, for which I
ST. BRIOCHE.
What does he mean?
CASCADA.
What does he mean?
MEN.
What does he mean?
What does he mean?
pp
DAN.
now ex_press my thanks, Is worth at least two thou_sand francs!
mf

DAN.
rit.
Yours the dance may be, If you'll give two thousand francs to me For char_i _ ty!
rit
mf
a tempo
CAMILLE.
Two thousand francs?
DAN.
It's go _ ing, _ go _ ing No ad _ vance?
ST. BRIOCHE.
Two thousand francs?
CASCADA.
(to ST. BRIOCHE.)
Two thousand francs? But for a dance?
MEN.
Two thousand francs?
Two thousand francs?
p
mf

(aside)
DAN.
It on - ly needs a lit-tle tact!
ST. B.
Two thousand francs!
(to CASCADA.)
He must be cracked!
CAS.
Two thousand francs!
MEN.
Two thousand francs!
Two thousand francs!
cresc.
mf
rit.
fz
(to SONIA.)
DAN.
Now you see, gracious la - dy, what I say! Your a - dor - ers
ST. B.
It's sim - ply sil - ly!
CAS.
Two thousand francs!
MEN.
Two thou-sand francs! It's sim - ply sil - ly!
Two thou-sand francs! It's sim - ply sil - ly!
pp

DAN.
all grow chil - ly, When you call on them to pay. They love you
p
DAN.
and a - dore, But love their mon - ey more. And that's the
mf
mf
(SONIA. turns away.)
CAMILLE.
(to NATALIE.)
DAN.
sort of man they raise In no - ble mod - ern days. I
rit
Allegro.
CAM.
can - not let him put me off so. It's two thou_sand francs — that I will
p
p

NATALIE.
(Seizes his arm.)
You're in love with her?
CAM.
(Surprised)
pay.
You told me so your-
pp
cre-
(draws him away.)
NAT.
You must come a-way!
(Exeunt.)
CAM.
-self
scen
do ff
rit.
Valse.
DANILO.
The last is gone, And you are free, And now,
pp
SONIA.
DAN.
mad-ame, per-haps You'll have the dance with me?
Now

DANILO.
SON.
I must de - cline!
The dance is mine, As you will al - low.
mf
p
SONIA.
Thank you, I do not dance —
At least, not now!
DANILO.
rit.
Hark to the mu - sic there at the ball!
Will you not fol - low its
rit.
mf
pp
DAN.
call?
Valse moderato.
8
pp

8
Ped.
SONIA.
No, I will not
Tempo di Valse.
8
mf
a tempo
p
Ped.
Ped.
Ped.
(He dances round her.)
mf con tenerezza
poco a poco cresc.
SONIA.
You're a ve - ry bad man,
But
mf

(She takes his arm.)
DANILO.
SON.
dance like an an - gel! I do what I can!
mf
f
ff
(The Curtain falls slowly.)
(Both dance off.)
sempre più
forte et molto animato
Presto.
fff
ff
ff
ff
ff
Ped.

END OF ACT I.

Act II.

Nº 7. OPENING CHORUS and SONG.-(Sonia.)

"VILIA."

5
SONIA.
I bid you
f
rit:
Allegretto moderato.
SON.
wait here for a min - ute, And you will see Our own Mar - so - vian dance, when
p
SON.
they be - gin it, Just as it would be, you un - der - stand, In our own na tive land.
pp

Vivace.
f
Ped.
f
f
ff
p
ff
p
ff
ff
p
ff
p
ff

Allegretto.
CHO.
Ah!
Ah!
Ah!
Allegretto.
f
CHO.
Ah!
Ah!
Ah!
CHO.
Ah!
Ah!
Ah!

CHO.
Ah!
Ah!
Ah!
CHO.
Ah!
Ah!
Ah!
CHO.
Ah!
Ah!
Ah!

Vivace.
CHO.
Hei - a - ho!
Down in dear Mar - so - via, that's the way we go, In the good old
Down in dear Mar - so - via, that's the way we go, In the good old
Vivace.
Ped.
Hei - a - ho!
fash - ion, danc - ing to and fro, Gai - ly sing - ing and
fash - ion, danc - ing to and fro, Gai - ly sing - ing and
Hei!
light - ly spring - ing, Maid - ens danc - ing and cym - bals
light - ly spring - ing, Maid - ens danc - ing and cym - bals

CHO.
Hei!
Hei!
ring - ing! Gai - ly sing - ing and light - ly spring - ing,
ring - ing! Gai - ly sing - ing and light - ly spring - ing,
ff
ff
p
CHO.
Hei! Down in
Maid - ens danc - ing and cym - bals ring - ing! Down in
Maid - ens danc - ing and cym - bals ring - ing! Down in
ff
p
ff
CHO.
dear Mar - so - via, So we go! Hei!
dear Mar - so - via, So we go! Hei!
dear Mar - so - via, So we go! Hei!
ff
ff

Allegretto moderato. SONIA.
Now sing our dear Mar-so-vian rhyme, A bal-lad made in
SON.
old-en time, The sto-ry all our chil-dren know, A-bout a Vil-ia long a-
SONG.-(Sonia.) "VILIA."
Allegretto
SON.
-go!
1. There once was a
wood-maid-en
SON.
Vil ia, A witch of the wood, A hunt-er be-held her a-
smiled, and no an-swer she gave, But beck-on'd him in-to the

SON.
_lone as she stood. The spell of her beau - - ty up -
shade of the cave; He nev - - er had known such a
p
SON.
_on him was laid; He look'd and he long'd for the
rap - tur _ ous bliss, No maid - en of mort - als so
pp rit.
SON.
mag - ic _ al maid! For a sud_den trem_or ran, Right thro' the love-be_wild _ er'd
sweet _ ly can kiss! As be_fore her feet he lay She vanish'd in the wood a _
Fl.
pp a tempo
SON.
man, And he sigh'd as a hap_less lov - er can.
_way, And he call'd vain_ly till his dy - ing day!
rit:
Fl.
mf rit:

SON.
"Vil - ia, O Vil - ia! the witch of the wood, Would I not
p
con Ped.
SON.
die for you, dear, if I could! Vil - ia, O Vil - ia, my
SON.
love and my bride!" Soft - ly and sad - ly he sigh'd.
p
CHO.
mf
Vil - ia, O Vil - ia! the witch of the wood!
mf
Vil - ia, O Vil - ia! the witch of the wood!
mf
Vil - ia, O Vil - ia! witch of the wood!
mf

CHO.
Would I not die for you, dear, if I could!
Would I not die for you, dear, if I could!
Would I not die for you, dear, if I could!
SON.
"Vil - ia, O Vil - ia, my love and my bride!"
SON.
Soft - ly and sad - ly he sigh'd.
1.
Allegretto.
SON.
2. The
mf
ppp
p
fz
f
pp

2.
SON.
sigh'd, Sad - ly he sigh'd Vil - - ia.
CHO.
For love he died.
For love he died.
For love he died.
2.
f
pp
f
8
Ped. * Ped. * Ped. * Ped. * Ped.
Vivace.
CHO.
f
Down in dear Mar - so - viä, thats the
f
Down in dear Mar - so - viä, that's the
Vivace.
8
p
f
* Ped.

CHO.
Hei - a - ho!
Hei - a - ho!
way we go, In the good old fash - ion dan - cing to and fro,
way we go, In the good old fash - ion dan - cing to and fro,
CHO.
Hei!
Gai - ly sing - ing and light - ly spring - ing! Maid - ens
Gai - ly sing - ing and light - ly spring - ing! Maid - ens
ff
p
ff
CHO.
Hei!
dan - cing and cym - bals ring - ing, Gai - ly
dan - cing and cym - bals ring - ing, Gai - ly
p
ff
ff

CHO.
Hei!
sing - ing and light - ly spring - ing, Maid - ens
sing - ing and light - ly spring - ing, Maid - ens
p
ff
CHO.
Hei! Down in
dan - cing and cym - bals ring - ing, Down in
dan - cing and cym - bals ring - ing, Down in
p
ff
CHO.
dear Mar - so - via, So we go! Hei!
dear Mar - so - via, So we go! Hei!
dear Mar - so - via, So we go! Hei!
ff

Nº 8. DUET.–(Sonia and Danilo.)

"THE CAVALIER."

SON.
Look up, maid - en, mark him well! Leave the dan - cers lone - ly,
pp
Ped. * Ped. * Ped. * Ped. *
SON.
He may like you, who can tell, If he sees you on - ly!
pp
fp
DANILO.
So she glan - ces shy and sly, And she meets the horse - man's eye!
pp
SONIA.
rit:
Not a word she says, but still, He can take her if he will!
mf
rit:
a tempo

Più lento.
SON.
Sil - ly, sil - ly cav - a - lier! He can nei - ther see nor hear;
pp
Ped.
rit:
Sil - ly, sil - ly horse - man! Ride up - on your course, man,
a tempo
Sil - ly, sil - ly cav - a - lier!
He that will not when he may,
mf
When he wills it shall have nay,
Sil - ly, sil - ly horse - man!
Ride up - on your course, man, Sil - ly, sil - ly cav - a - lier!
p
mf

Animato.
p
ff
Allegretto.
ff
fz
Ped.
SONIA.
Hal_lo! Here he comes a_gain! See his charg_er wheel_ing!
pp
SON.
Now he seems a love-lorn swain, Beg_ging and ap - peal_ing!
pp
mf

SON.
But the maid - en, calm and cool, Sings and does - n't care now!
pp
Ped. * Ped. * Ped. * Ped. *
SON.
"Cav - a - lier, if you're a fool I am not,— so there now!"
pp
fp
DANILO.
So the horse-man laughs,"All right!" If you won't,why,then good - night!
pp
DAN.
Pret - ty maid - en, now good-bye,— Take an-oth - er, so will I!
mf
rit:
rit:
a tempo
SONIA. Più lento.
Sil - ly, sil - ly cav - a - lier! You can nei-ther see nor hear!
Più lento.
pp
Ped. * Ped. *

SON.
DAN.
rit:
a tempo
Sil_ly sil_ly horse-man! Ride up_on your course, man! Sil_ly, sil_ly cav - a - lier!
Clev_er clev_er horse-man! That's the pro_per course, man! Clev_er, clev_er cav - a - lier!
He that will not when he may,
You may take it as you may,
When he wills it, shall have nay!
I shall love and ride a - way!
Sil_ly, sil_ly horse - man, Ride up_on your course, man, Sil_ly, sil_ly cav - a - lier!
Clev_er, clev_er horse - man, That's the pro_per course, man, Clev_er, clev_er cav - a - lier!
p
mf
pp
pp rit:
mf a tempo
mf
Ped.

Allegro moderato.
mf
Ped.
(DANILO saluts and exit.)
ff
(SONIA moves after him.)
(She stops.)
SONIA.
rit:
Sil - ly, sil - ly horse-man! Ride up - on your course, man! Sil - ly, sil - ly cav - a - lier!
Allegro.
Allegro.
rit:
f
ff

No. 9. MARCH-SEPTET.

"WOMEN."

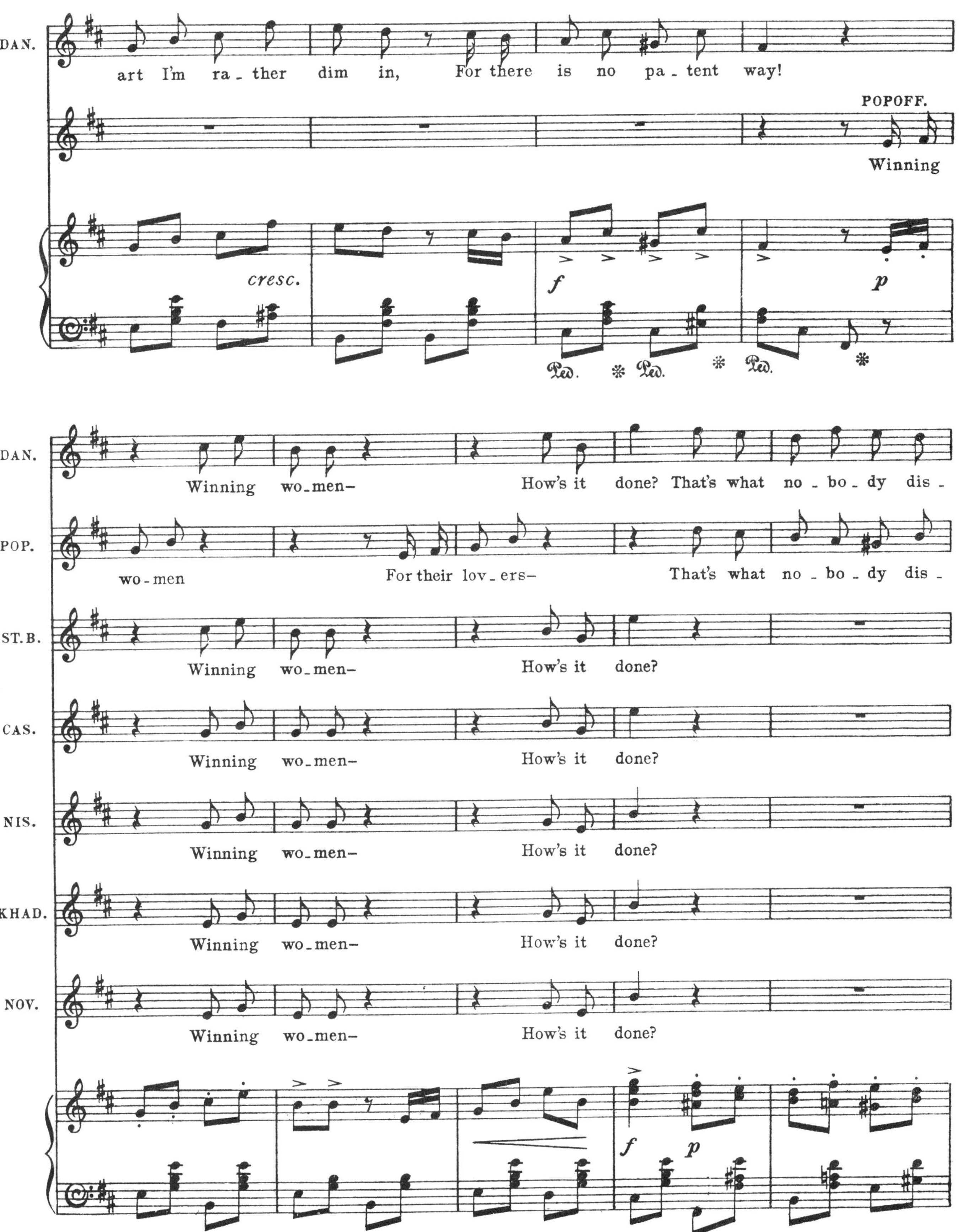
DAN.
art I'm ra_ther dim in, For there is no pa_tent way!
POPOFF.
Winning
cresc.
f
p
Ped. * Ped. * Ped. *
DAN.
Winning wo_men– How's it done? That's what no_bo_dy dis_
POP.
wo_men For their lov_ers– That's what no_bo_dy dis_
ST. B.
Winning wo_men– How's it done?
CAS.
Winning wo_men– How's it done?
NIS.
Winning wo_men– How's it done?
KHAD.
Winning wo_men– How's it done?
NOV.
Winning wo_men– How's it done?
f p

DAN.
POP.
ST. B.
CAS.
NIS.
KHAD.
NOV.
-cov - ers, Not ev-en an Ed-i-son! With one you have to flirt and flat-ter-
-cov - ers, Not ev-en an Ed-i-son!
Not ev-en an Ed-i-son!
So and so and so and so!
So and so and so and so! And look un-ut-ter-a-bly at her- So and so and
So and so and

DAN.
so and so!
So and so and so and so!
POP.
so and so!
So and so and so and so!
ST. B.
so and so! An - o - ther likes you when you blus_ter-
So and so and so and so!
CAS.
so and so!
So and so and so and so! And
NIS.
so and so!
So and so and so and so!
KHAD.
so and so!
So and so and so and so!
NOV.
so and so!
So and so and so and so!
mf
DAN.
So and so and so and so! One
POP.
So and so and so and so!
ST. B.
So and so and so and so!
CAS.
while you beat her you can trust her-
So and so and so and so!
NIS.
So and so and so and so!
KHAD.
So and so and so and so!
NOV.
So and so and so and so!
mf

DAN.
asks for ten - der - ness un - flag - ging- So and so and so and so!
POP.
So and so and so and so! An -
ST. B.
So and so and so and so!
CAS.
So and so and so and so!
NIS.
So and so and so and so!
KHAD.
So and so and so and so!
NOV.
So and so and so and so!
p
DAN.
So and so and so and so!
POP.
- o - ther's al - ways rag - ging, nag - ging- So and so and so and so!
ST. B.
So and so and so and so!
CAS.
So and so and so and so! An -
NIS.
So and so and so and so!
KHAD.
So and so and so and so!
NOV.
So and so and so and so!
mf

Animato.
rit.
rall.
DAN.
So and so and so and so! And o-ther things they
POP.
So and so and so and so! And o-ther things they
ST. B.
So and so and so and so! And o-ther things they
CAS.
-o-ther likes in-ces-sant laugh-ter- So and so and so and so! And o-ther things they
NIS.
So and so and so and so!
KHAD.
So and so and so and so!
NOV.
So and so and so and so!
Animato.
f rit.
p
rall.
Ped.
rit.
a tempo
DAN.
ask for af-ter- So and so and so and so! You may
POP.
ask for af-ter- So and so and so and so! You may
ST. B.
ask for af-ter- So and so and so and so!
CAS.
ask for af-ter- So and so and so and so!
NIS.
So and so and so and so!
KHAD.
So and so and so and so!
NOV.
So and so and so and so!
pp
rit.
p a tempo
Ped.

TRIO.
Tempo I.
DAN.
stu - dy her ways as you can; But a wo - man's too
POP.
stu - dy her ways as you can; But a wo - man's too
ST. B.
Oh, the women! Bless the women!
CAS.
Oh, the women! Bless the women!
NIS.
Oh, the women! Bless the women!
KHAD.
Oh, the women! Bless the women!
NOV.
Oh, the women! Bless the women!
Tempo I.
p
DAN.
much for a man! It is deep - er than div - ing for
POP.
much for a man! It is deep - er than div - ing for
ST. B.
Oh, the women! Hang the women!
CAS.
Oh, the women! Hang the women!
NIS.
Oh, the women! Hang the women!
KHAD.
Oh, the women! Hang the women!
NOV.
Oh, the women! Hang the women!

DAN.
pearls Court_ing girls, girls, girls, girls, girls! With her
POP.
pearls Court_ing girls, girls, girls, girls, girls! With her
ST. B.
Girls, girls, girls, girls!
CAS.
Girls, girls, girls, girls!
NIS.
Girls, girls, girls, girls!
KHAD.
Girls, girls, girls, girls!
NOV.
Girls, girls, girls, girls!
ff
p
DAN.
fair flax_en hair, eyes of blue, She's a long way too know _ ing for
POP.
fair flax_en hair, eyes of blue, She's a long way too know _ ing for
ST. B.
Oh, the women! Darling women!
CAS.
Oh, the women! Darling women!
NIS.
Oh, the women! Darling women!
KHAD.
Oh, the women! Darling women!
NOV.
Oh, the women! Darling women!
p

DAN.
you. She is dark, or she's fair, She may smile or may

POP.
you. She is dark, or she's fair, She may smile or may

ST. B.
Oh, the women! Blow the women!

CAS.
Oh, the women! Blow the women!

NIS.
Oh, the women! Blow the women!

KHAD.
Oh, the women! Blow the women!

NOV.
Oh, the women! Blow the women!

cre - - - scen - - - do

DAN.
frown– Nev - er mind, you will get done brown!

POP.
frown– Nev - er mind, you will get done brown!

ST. B.

CAS.

NIS.

KHAD.

NOV.

f

fz

DAN.
POP.
ST.B.
CAS.
NIS.
KHAD.
NOV.
Wo_men, wo_men, wo_men, wo_men, wo_men, wo_men, ah!
Wo_men, wo_men, wo_men, wo_men, wo_men, wo_men,
f
Ah!
rit.
ff
You may
wo_men, wo_men, wo_men, wo_men, wo_men, wo_men, ah! You may
ah!
molto cresc.

DAN.
stu - dy her ways as you can, But a wo - man's too
POP.
stu - dy her ways as you can, But a wo - man's too
ST. B.
stu - dy her ways as you can, But a wo - man's too
CAS.
stu - dy her ways as you can, But a wo - man's too
NIS.
stu - dy her ways as you can, But a wo - man's too
KHAD.
stu - dy her ways as you can, But a wo - man's too
NOV.
stu - dy her ways as you can, But a wo - man's too
Ped.
*
DAN.
much for a man! It is deep - er than div - ing for
POP.
much for a man! It is deep - er than div - ing for
ST. B.
much for a man! It is deep - er than div - ing for
CAS.
much for a man! It is deep - er than div - ing for
NIS.
much for a man! It is deep - er than div - ing for
KHAD.
much for a man! It is deep - er than div - ing for
NOV.
much for a man! It is deep - er than div - ing for
mf
Ped.
*

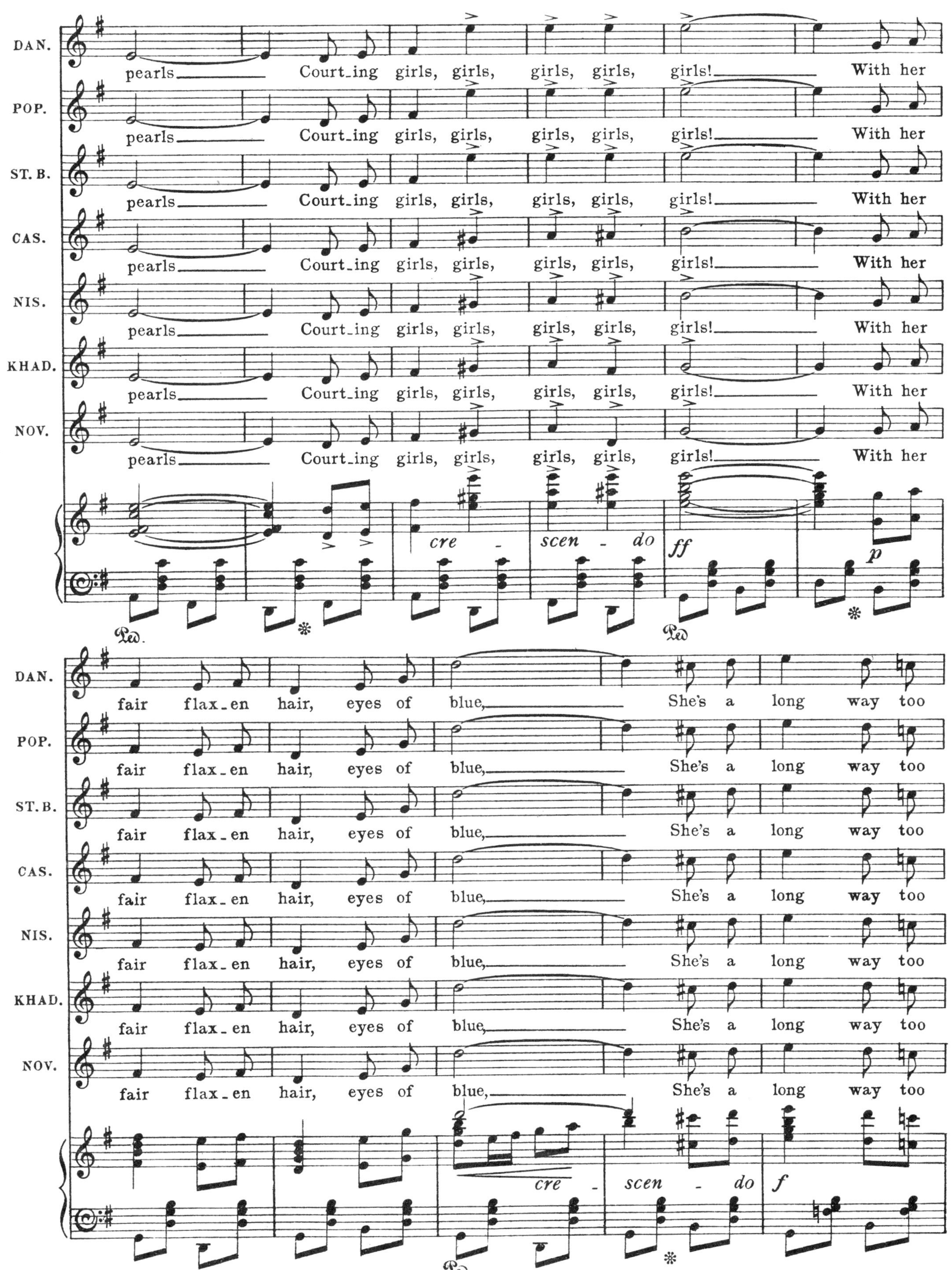
DAN.
POP.
ST. B.
CAS.
NIS.
KHAD.
NOV.
pearls Court_ing girls, girls, girls, girls, girls! With her
cre - scen - do ff p
fair flax_en hair, eyes of blue, She's a long way too
cre - scen - do f

DAN.
know - ing for you! She is dark, or she's fair, She may

POP.
know - ing for you! She is dark, or she's fair, She may

ST. B.
know - ing for you! She is dark, or she's fair, She may

CAS.
know - ing for you! She is dark, or she's fair, She may

NIS.
know - ing for you! She is dark, or she's fair, She may

KHAD.
know - ing for you! She is dark, or she's fair, She may

NOV.
know - ing for you! She is dark, or she's fair, She may

ff

Ped. * Ped. *

DAN.
smile or may frown– Nev - er mind, you will get done brown! ppp You may

POP.
smile or may frown– Nev - er mind, you will get done brown! ppp You may

ST. B.
smile or may frown– Nev - er mind, you will get done brown!

CAS.
smile or may frown– Nev - er mind, you will get done brown!

NIS.
smile or may frown– Nev - er mind, you will get done brown!

KHAD.
smile or may frown– Nev - er mind, you will get done brown!

NOV.
smile or may frown– Nev - er mind, you will get done brown!

ppp

Ped. * Ped. * Ped. * Ped. *

DAN.
stu - dy her ways as you can, But a wo - man's too
POP.
stu - dy her ways as you can, But a wo - man's too
ST. B.
Wo - men!
GAS.
Women!
NIS.
Wo_men!
KHAD.
Women!
NOV.
Women!
sempre leggiero
DAN.
much for a man! It is deep - er than div - ing for
POP.
much for a man! It is deep - er than div - ing for
ST. B.
Wom - en!
GAS.
Women!
NIS.
Women!
KHAD.
Women!
NOV.
Women!

DAN. pearls, Courting girls, girls, girls, girls, girls With her *pp*

POP. pearls, Courting girls, girls, girls, girls, girls With her *pp*

ST. B. *f* Women! Girls, girls, girls, girls With her *pp*

GAS. *f* Women! Girls, girls, girls, girls With her *pp*

NIS. *f* Women! Girls, girls, girls, girls With her *pp*

KHAD. *f* Women! Girls, girls, girls, girls With her *pp*

NOV. Girls, girls, girls, girls, girls With her *pp*

cre - scen - do. ff *pp*

DAN. fair flaxen hair, eyes of blue, She's a long way too

POP. fair flaxen hair, eyes of blue, She's a long way too

ST. B. fair flaxen hair, eyes of blue, She's a long way too

GAS. fair flaxen hair, eyes of blue, She's a long way too

NIS. fair flaxen hair, eyes of blue, She's a long way too

KHAD. fair flaxen hair, eyes of blue, She's a long way too

NOV. fair flaxen hair, eyes of blue, She's a long way too

cresc.

DAN. know - ing for you! She is dark, or she's fair, She may

POP. know - ing for you! She is dark, or she's fair, She may

T. B. know - ing for you! She is dark, or she's fair, She may

GAS. know - ing for you! She is dark, or she's fair, She may

NIS. know - ing for you! She is dark, or she's fair, She may

KHAD. know - ing for you! She is dark, or she's fair, She may

NOV. know - ing for you! She is dark, or she's fair, She may

f *cre -*

DAN. smile or may frown– Nev - er mind, You will get done brown!

POP. smile or may frown– Nev - er mind, You will get done brown!

T. B. smile or may frown– Nev - er mind, You will get done brown!

GAS. smile or may frown– Nev - er mind, You will get done brown!

NIS. smile or may frown– Nev - er mind, You will get done brown!

KHAD. smile or may frown– Nev - er mind, You will get done brown!

NOV. smile or may frown– Nev - er mind, You will get done brown!

- scen - - do *ff* *fz*

Nº 10. DUET. (Sonia and Danilo.)

p
Ped.
pp
Ped.
p
mf
p
rit.
pp
Vivace.
f
Ped.

p
sempre più animato et crescendo
f
f
ff
ff
ff

II.
Allegretto moderato.
p
mf
DANILO.
Allegretto.
He'll take you to Max-
DAN.
-im's where fun and frol-ic beams!
pp
pp

Moderato.
Tempo di Valse moderato.
pp
con Ped.
Ped.
Ped.
Ped.
p rit.

Valse lente.
Ped.
Ped.
Ped.
pp
Tempo di Valse.
SON.
(closed lips)
DAN.
Tempo di Valse.
pp
SON.
DAN.

SON.
DAN.
Ped.
SON.
DAN.
SON.
DAN.
f
f

Nº 11. DUET. (Natalie and Camille.) and ROMANCE. (Camille.)

"LOVE IN MY HEART."

NATALIE.
rit.
Moderato
Oh, do not doubt I feel it
tr
rit.
pp
NAT.
too! With_out your love life will be hol _ low; But
fz
NAT.
hon _ our tells me what to do, And when it calls me I must
pp
mf
NAT.
fol _ low.
Ah!
CAMILLE.
Then may I nev _ er hope to meet you?
mf

animato
NAT.
do not tor_ture me, I en_treat you!
CAM.
No more I say— I will o_bey.
p
p animato
It is my heart, my love, that I fear!
Ah!
mf
You should not have ask'd me!
let me kiss you!
For_give, for_give me, dear!
f
p
mf

Romance. (CAMILLE) "Love in my heart."
Allegretto.
CAMILLE.
Love in my heart a - wak - - - ing, A rose - bud in the May,
In - to full beau - ty break - ing, Be - came a rose to - day.
I hard - ly mark'd it bud - - ding To - wards the sun a -
CAM.
rit.
pp
p
mf
Ped.

CAM.
-bove
Un-til it op-en'd, flood-ing My
p
mf
p
Ped.
rit.
heart with joy of love.
a tempo
And now I know my
pp rit.
p
pp a tempo
tranquillo
Con Ped.
pas-sion, It can-not but be told!
The
f
rose that love can fash-ion Shall bloom in spite of
rit.
pp
rit.

animato
CAM.
cold. My heart with song is ring - ing Like
p animato
cres -
CAM.
birds that greet the sun, I know as I am
- cen - - - do - - - - - - f
CAM.
sing - ing The day of love is won! Oh
CAM.
an - swer to my sing - ing, And say my love is
cresc.
ff

Allegretto.
NATALIE.
Oh, Ca - mille!
CAM.
won!
Nat - a - lie!
p
dim.
animato
NAT.
Ah! leave me, pray! I
animato
cres - - - - - - - cen - - - - do -
NAT.
know not what I shall do or say!
8
CAMILLE.
Good - bye, then, my dar - ling— Give me one last
f

NATALIE.
rit.
No, not here!
CAM.
rit.
kiss!
Più lento
See, there's a lit - tle ar - bour
8
rit.
pp Più lento
CAM.
there— It can hear a kiss and will not tell!
CAM.
Our ten-der se-cret it may share When we bid a lov-er's
mf
CAM.
last fare - well!
animato
Tho' 'tis dark a -
p animato

CAM.
round, There will love's light be found
f
rit.
lento
rit.
CAM.
Come to the lit-tle ar-bour here There is no-thing there to
p lento
rit.
Moderato.
NATALIE.
CAM.
fear, My dear!
I
pp
NAT.
ought not Yet I can-not re-sist you!

NATALIE.
CAMILLE.
No one will hear us?
Come to the lit_tle ar_bour here. Not a soul will know I
mf
NAT.
CAM.
I must not hear! Though 'tis_dark a_
kissed you, dear! Though 'tis_dark a_
p
_round, There will love's light be found
f
rit.

NAT.
CAM.
rit.
Come to the lit_tle ar_bour here— There is no_thing there to
p a tempo
rit.
Allegro.
My dear!
fear, My dear!
Allegro.
p
ff

Nº 12. FINALE.–ACT II.

NATALIE.
I'm here, dear!
DAN.
ve - ry much too clear!
POPOFF.
Then where can be my wife?
NATALIE.
What's go_ing on? I'd like to know!
CAMILLE.
There's
POPOFF.
Well, I'm sim_ply blowed!
DANILO.
Ha! Son_ia and Camille!
mf
CAM.
no_thing wrong! Be still!
POPOFF.
I saw a la - dy in there just be_fore- Yes, through the
p
p

SONIA.
You are a sly Am_bas_sa_dor!
DANILO.
That is what he's for!
POP.
key_hole of the door.
I hard_ly could be - lieve my
POP.
ve - ry ears,
When love un - end - ing
that fel _ low
mf
SONIA.
The la - dy- that was I!
DANILO.
You, Son_ia!
POP.
swore!
POPOFF.
I would have
p

SONIA.
My dear - est Ca-mille, con -
POP.
sworn it was my wife, you know!
SON.
- fess it was so!
SONIA.
Well,
NATALIE.
Al-though it saves— me, it fills me with woe!
CAMILLE.
Al-though it saves— her, I speak it in woe!
DANILO.
With rage and jeal-ous - y my heart is a - glow!
KHADJA.
I can't be - lieve— it! Oh, no! Oh, no!
NISCH.
I man-aged ev - 'ry-thing, and got up the show!
mf
p

Più lento.
SON.
since the Am_bas - sa - dor sees fit To lis - ten and spy at the ar_bour door
mf
SON.
rit.
Pray tell them all the whole truth of it, Re - peat_ing what you said in
p
rit.
pp
SON.
there, just be_fore!
CAMILLE.
Must I de_clare it?
DANILO.
And I have to bear it?
mf
CAMILLE.
Your Ex_cellency, as I have to o_bey, All that I told her a_gain I will
mf
3
p
p
mf

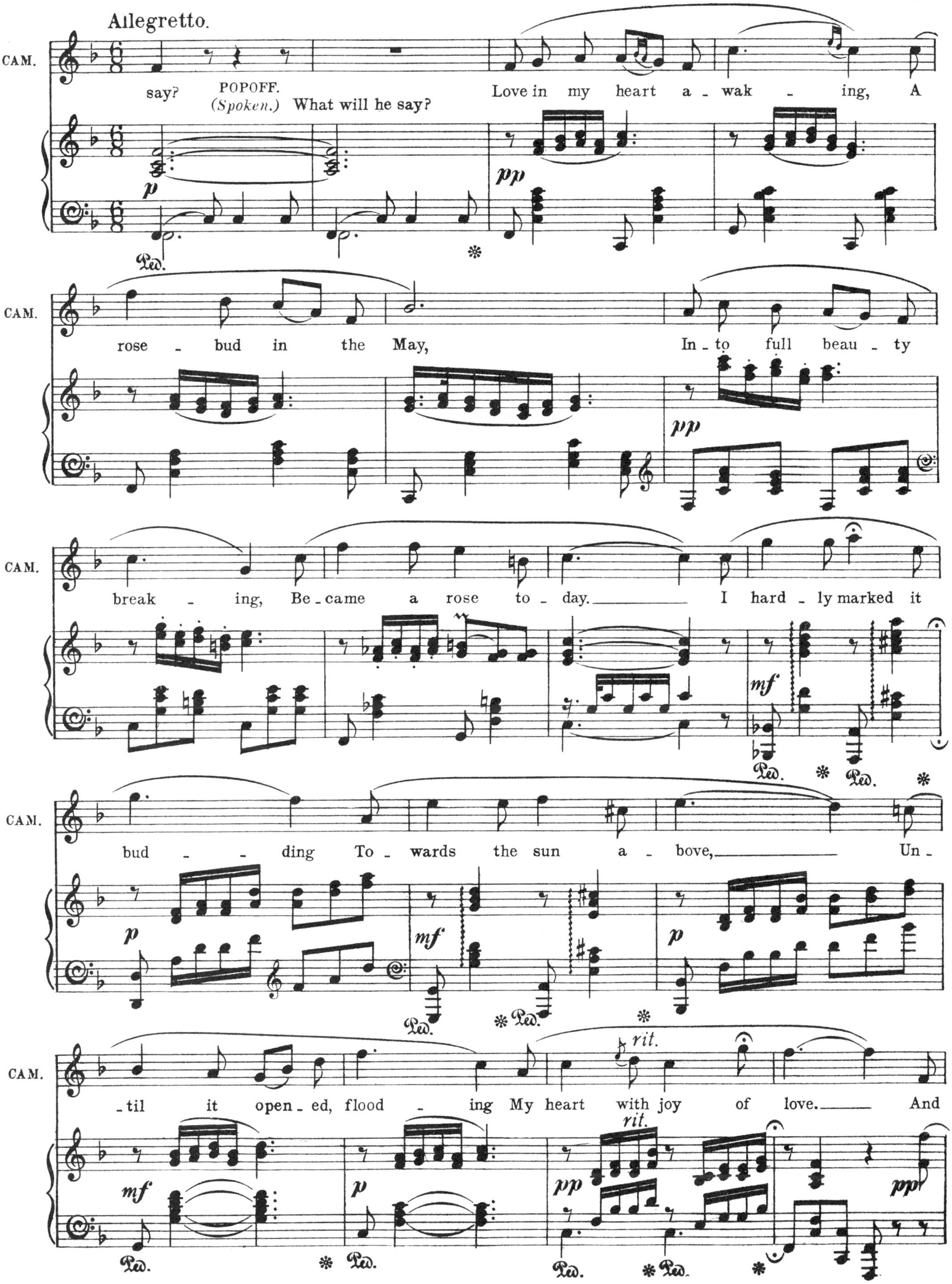

Allegretto.

CAM. say?

POPOFF. (*Spoken.*) What will he say?

CAM. Love in my heart a - wak - ing, A rose - bud in the May, In - to full beau - ty break - ing, Be - came a rose to - day. I hard - ly marked it bud - ding To - wards the sun a - bove, Un - til it open - ed, flood - ing My heart with joy of love. And

SONIA.
His face is quite a sight to
NATALIE.
It al - most breaks my heart to
CAM.
now I know my pas - sion, It can - not but be
NISCH.
This is a sud - den pas - sion!
KHADJA.
She does - n't seem to scorn his
a tempo
f
Ped.
* Ped.
*
SON.
see!
He thinks the song is
NAT.
see
He looks at her as
CAM.
told
The rose that love can fash - ion Shall
NIS.
Now we are nice - ly sold!
But he's a man of
KHAD.
pas - sion,
She flirts with
Ped.
* Ped.
*

SON.
NAT.
CAM.
NIS.
KHAD.
rit.
meant for me! Ah,
once at me! That
bloom in spite of cold My heart with joy is
fash - ion, He is af - ter gold! In half a
him in reck - less fash - ion! Our wi - dow's
pp
rit.
a tempo
mf
no - ble Prince, I think I have won;
song, whose e - cho hard - ly is done, He sings it now
ring - ing Like birds that greet the sun I know as I am
min - ute- He has wooed and won! He is the man to
ra - ther hot— I'm glad my wife is not!
cresc.
f

SON.
NAT.
CAM.
NIS.
KHAD.
You'll have to speak be - fore you've done!
as if he loved an - oth - er one!
sing - ing The day of love is won Oh,
win it, And we are sim - ply done!
If I should catch him sing - ing I soon would spoil his fun
Ah, no - ble Prince, I've fair - ly
Has love an end so soon be - fore 'tis well be -
an - swer back my sing - ing, And say my love is
He is the man to win it all, And we are sim - ply
By neat - ly wing - ing Him with sword or
cresc.
ff

SON.
won — Yes, I've won!
NAT.
- gun? All is done!
CAM.
won Love is won!
NIS.
done We are done!
KHAD.
gun! Oh, what fun!
ff
ff
ffz
Ped.
Allegro.
SONIA. (Spoken.) Now, ladies and gentlemen, you shall know what was arranged in the arbour.
(aside.) It's neck or nothing! Now I play my trump card!
fp
f
cresc.
SONIA.
Al - low me to
f

(looks at DANILO.)
SON.
tell you, if it won't bore you_
A pair en_
CHO.
Oh, no! Oh, no!
Oh, no! Oh, no!
Oh, no! Oh, no!
SON.
gaged you see be_fore you!
This gen_tle_man_
NATALIE.
Oh,
CAMILLE.
What I?

SON.
and my most hum - ble self?
NAT.
Heaven!
Un - true!
CAM.
I?
Un - true!
DAN.
Not that!
Un - true!
POP.
What now?
Un -
CHO.
Ah! what a piece of news!
Ah! what a piece of news!
Ah! what a piece of news!
POP.
- true!
SONIA.
I
Allegro.
thought that bit of news would do!

DAN.
He takes her for her cur_sed mon _ ey!
POP.
He's got a_way with all our mon _ ey!
CHO.
Con_grat_u_la _ tions!
Con_grat_u_la _ tions!
Con_grat_u_la _ tions!
SONIA (to CAMILLE.)
Be_ware, or she is the
CAMILLE (to SONIA.)
That goes too far! I real_ly am sur_prised—
f

SON.
one com-pro-mised!
Why should-n't
(to CAMILLE.)
NAT.
Real - ly, do you mean-
POP.
You real-ly mean it?
p
SON.
I?
(to DANILO.)
You won't!
DANILO.
rit.
DAN.
molto rit.
Oh no! why should I raise ob -
POP.
I won't al-low it, nor the Prince!
colla voce
molto rit.
DAN.
-jec-tions so? I give you my pa-ter-nal bless-ing! On-
f
p

Andante.
SON.
What do you think?
DAN.
-ly I think—
Love when you
may, Pro-pose but
Andante.
f
pp
DAN.
sel-dom,
Mar-ry not at
all!
Mazurka moderato.
CAMILLE.
Tho' marriage in the old-en way
p
con Ped.
CAM.
Is whol-ly out-of-date to-day,
And as our friend has told us,
CAM.
Quite un-dip-lo-mat-ic,
Yet if the la-dy mar-ries me,
p

CAM.
A mod-ern wed-ding it will be, I prom-ise,— I prom-ise
In a style en-phat-ic! We make a lit-tle change of name,
p
In-stead of two, we have the same, Just like a sis-ter and a
brith-er; But when the ce-re-mo-ny's done, Wher-ev-er-
rit.
pp rit.
Ped.

Allegretto moderato.
CAM.
you may meet with one, You won't ex - pect to find the
oth - er! In fact, you'll find it safe to state, We are a
mf
pair en-tire-ly up - to-date!
Vivace.
ff
SONIA.
My
p

Tempo di Marcia.
SON.
mar - riage will be one ar - ranged, Quite in the mod - ern
fz
style; My name is all that will be changed—
p
That's in the mod - ern style! And as I shan't be
mf
on the shelf, Not for a lit - tle while, I'll

SON.
rit.
Vivace.
go a-head and please my-self, Quite in the mod-ern style! I am
p
rit.
free, so, tra-la-la-la-la-la! Still I'll be so,
mf
tra-la-la-la-la-la! And men may come and men may go, They
cre-scen-do
will not break my heart, oh, no! Oh, no, no, no, no, no, no, no, no,
f
fz

SON.
no! La, la, la, la, la, la, la, la, la, la! la, la, la, la,
NATALIE.
La, la, la, la, la, la, la, la, la, la!
SYLVAINE.
She is free, so tra - la-la-la - la - la, Still she'll
OLGA.
She is free, so tra - la-la-la - la - la, Still she'll
PRASKOVIA.
She is free, so tra - la-la-la - la - la, Still she'll
CAMILLE.
She is free, so tra - la-la-la - la - la, Still she'll
POPOFF.
She is free, so tra - la-la-la - la - la, Still she'll
KHADJA.
She is free, so tra - la-la-la - la - la, Still she'll
NOVIKOVICH.
She is free, so tra - la-la-la - la - la, Still she'll
She is free, so tra - la-la-la - la - la, Still she'll
CHO.
She is free, so tra - la-la-la - la - la, Still she'll
She is free, so tra - la-la-la - la - la, Still she'll
f
p
f

SON.
la, la, la, la, la, la!
NAT.
la, la, la, la, la, la, la, la, la, la!
SYL.
be, so tra - la - la - la - la - la And men may come and men may
OLGA.
be, so tra - la - la - la - la - la And men may come and men may
PRAS.
be, so tra - la - la - la - la - la And men may come and men may
CAM.
be, so tra - la - la - la - la - la And men may come and men may
POP.
be, so tra - la - la - la - la - la And men may come and men may
KHAD.
be, so tra - la - la - la - la - la And men may come and men may
NOV.
be, so tra - la - la - la - la - la And men may come and men may
CHO.
be, so tra - la - la - la - la - la And men may come and men may
be, so tra - la - la - la - la - la And men may come and men may
be, so tra - la - la - la - la - la And men may come and men may
p
cre - - - - scen -
Ped. * Ped. *

SON.
Go They will not break my heart. No!
NAT.
Go They will not break her heart. No! And
SYL.
go, They will not break her heart, Oh no, oh, no!
OLGA.
go, They will not break her heart, Oh no, oh, no!
PRAS.
go, They will not break her heart. No!
CAM.
go, They will not break her heart, Oh no, oh, no!
POP.
go, They will not break her heart, Oh no, oh, no!
KHAD.
go, They will not break her heart, Oh no, oh, no!
NOV.
go, They will not break her heart, Oh no, oh, no!
CHO.
go, They will not break her heart, Oh no, oh, no!
go, They will not break her heart, Oh no, oh, no!
go, They will not break her heart, Oh no, oh, no!
do
f
p

Tempo di Marcia.

Vivace.
SON.
That's the la - test— tra - la-la-la - la - la! Up to
NAT.
That's the la - test— tra - la-la-la - la - la! Up to
Vivace.
f
p
mf
SON.
da - test— tra - la-la-la-la - la, Do what you like, but don't be slow, And
NAT.
da - test— tra - la-la-la-la - la, Do what you like, but don't be slow, And
p
cresc.
SON.
no - bo - dy will mind, oh no! Oh no, no, no, no, no, no, no, no,
NAT.
no - bo - dy will mind, oh no! Oh no, no, no, no, no, no, no, no,
f
fz

SON.
no. La, la, la, la, la, la, la, la, la, la! la, la, la, la,
NAT.
no. La, la, la, la, la, la, la, la, la, la!
SYLVAINE.
That's the la - test tra-la-la-la-la-la! Up to
OLGA.
That's the la - test tra-la-la-la-la-la! Up to
PRASKOVIA.
That's the la - test tra-la-la-la-la-la! Up to
CAMILLE.
That's the la - test tra-la-la-la-la-la! Up to
POPOFF.
That's the la - test tra-la-la-la-la-la! Up to
KHADJA.
That's the la - test tra-la-la-la-la-la! Up to
NOVIKOVICH.
That's the la - test tra-la-la-la-la-la! Up to
CHO.
That's the la - test tra-la-la-la-la-la! Up to
That's the la - test tra-la-la-la-la-la! Up to
That's the la - test tra-la-la-la-la-la! Up to

SON.
la, la, la, la, la, la!
NAT.
la, la, la, la, la, la, la, la, la, la.
SYL.
da - test— tra - la - la - la - la - la! Do what you like, but don't be
OLGA.
da - test— tra - la - la - la - la - la! Do what you like, but don't be
PRAS.
da - test— tra - la - la - la - la - la! Do what you like, but don't be
CAM.
da - test— tra - la - la - la - la - la! Do what you like, but don't be
POP.
da - test— tra - la - la - la - la - la! Do what you like, but don't be
KHAD.
da - test— tra - la - la - la - la - la! Do what you like, but don't be
NOV.
da - test— tra - la - la - la - la - la! Do what you like, but don't be
CHO.
da - test— tra - la - la - la - la - la! Do what you like, but don't be
da - test— tra - la - la - la - la - la! Do what you like, but don't be
da - test— tra - la - la - la - la - la! Do what you like, but don't be
p
cresc.
Ped.
Ped.

SON.
No And no-bo-dy will mind, No!
NAT.
No And no-bo-dy will mind, No!
SYL.
slow, And no-bo-dy will mind, oh no! Oh no!
OLGA.
slow, And no-bo-dy will mind, oh no! Oh no!
PRAS.
slow, And no-bo-dy will mind, No!
DANILO. Spoken.
CAM.
Oh! the wo-man's cool as-
DAN.
slow, And no-bo-dy will mind, oh no! Oh no!
POP.
slow, And no-bo-dy will mind, oh no! Oh no!
KHAD.
slow, And no-bo-dy will mind, oh no! Oh no!
NOV.
slow, And no-bo-dy will mind, oh no! Oh no!
CHO.
slow, And no-bo-dy will mind, oh no! Oh no!
slow, And no-bo-dy will mind, oh no! Oh no!
slow, And no-bo-dy will mind, oh no! Oh no!
cresc.
f
ff
Ped.
Ped.

DAN.
_sur_ance Vex_es me be_yond en _ dur_ance! I will speak!
rit.
f
DAN.
lento.
for it must out! But I can_not speak the whole Of the an_ger in my
f
mf
DAN.
Allegro moderato.
soul— Let me keep my self - con - trol! To grace the
p
p
DAN.
wed - - ding, fair ma_dame, Pray can I tell a lit_tle

SONIA. (coldly)
Oh, do! I'll lis_ten till the end! As_ you
DAN.
sto - ry?
mf
SON.
see, I ea_ger_ly at_tend. Won't you tell us?
DANILO.
I will
DAN.
rit.
tell you. There once were two Prin - ces' chil - - dren Who
Tempo di Valse lento.
mf
rit.
pp
DAN.
loved when the world was so young, But nev_er were hap_py to_
p

DAN.
-geth - - er; It's just as the po - et has sung.
Ped.
DAN.
The Prince nev - er told of his pas - sion, For ve - ry good
mf
Ped.
DAN.
rea - son, no doubt; And so the Prin - cess was un -
pp
Ped.
rit.
DAN.
hap - py Be - cause he would nev - er speak out! And
rit.
Ped.

DAN.
then the Prin - cess was so cru - el, When he would not ask for her
pp
Ped.
hand, She prom-ised to mar-ry a - noth-er— 'Twas
mf
p
more than the Prince could stand! "Most gracious and beau-ti-ful
a tempo
pp rit.
mf
pp
la - dy, It was not a good thing to do! All

DAN.
wom-en are faith-less and fic-kle, And on-ly a wom-an are
mf
p rit.
DAN.
Valse.
you! But do you sup-pose I am sor-ry? Ha,
a tempo
pp
Ped.
DAN.
ha! I don't mean to cry! I shall not go dream-ing a-
p
Ped.
DAN.
-bout you," That's what the Prince said, and not I! And
Ped.

DAN.
thus said the Prince as he end - ed,
"There, mar-ry, I've
fin - ish'd with you!"
With that the Prince cool - ly de -
- part - ed,
And so will I now—
A -
Allegro.
SONIA.
Andante.
Where are you go - ing, then?
dieu!
poco più animato
p
pp
f
mf

DANILO.
Where I won't see you a_gain!
f
Allegretto.
DAN.
I'll go off to Max_im's— I've done with lovers' dreams. The girls will laugh and
p
DAN.
greet me, They will not trick and cheat me! Lo_lo, Do_do, Jou_jou, Clo_clo, Mar_got, Frou_
p
SONIA.
He loves me I'm sure of it
DAN.
frou; I'm go_ing off to Max_im's And you may go to—
f

Molto Allegro.
Vivace.
SON.
now.
He loves
ff
mf
me, so tra-la-la-la-la-la! We shall see, so
p
mf
tra-la-la-la-la-la! Where-ev-er he may try to go, He
p
cresc.
won't es-cape from me, oh, no! Oh, no, no, no, no, no, no, no, no,
f
fz

SON.
no! La, la, la, la, la, la, la, la, la, la!
la, la, la, la, la, la, la, la, la, la!
NAT.
La, la, la, la, la, la, la, la, la, la!
la, la, la, la,
SYL.
She is free, so tra-la-la-la-la-la! Still she'll be, so tra-la-la-la-la-
OLGA.
She is free, so tra-la-la-la-la-la! Still she'll be, so tra-la-la-la-la-
PRAS.
She is free, so tra-la-la-la-la-la! Still she'll be, so tra-la-la-la-la-
CAM.
She is free, so tra-la-la-la-la-la! Still she'll be, so tra-la-la-la-la-
POP.
She is free, so tra-la-la-la-la-la! Still she'll be, so tra-la-la-la-la-
CAS.
She is free, so tra-la-la-la-la-la! Still she'll be, so tra-la-la-la-la-
KHAD.
She is free, so tra-la-la-la-la-la! Still she'll be, so tra-la-la-la-la-
NOV.
She is free, so tra-la-la-la-la-la! Still she'll be, so tra-la-la-la-la-
CHO.
She is free, so tra-la-la-la-la-la! Still she'll be, so tra-la-la-la-la-
She is free, so tra-la-la-la-la-la! Still she'll be, so tra-la-la-la-la-
She is free, so tra-la-la-la-la-la! Still she'll be, so tra-la-la-la-la-
f
p
f
p

SON.
No they will not break my heart,
NAT.
la, la, la, la, la, la!
No they will not break her heart, oh no, Oh
SYL.
-la! And men may come and men may go, They will not break her heart, oh no, Oh
OLGA.
-la! And men may come and men may go, They will not break her heart, oh no, Oh
PRAS.
-la! And men may come and men may go, They will not break her heart, oh no, Oh
CAM.
-la! And men may come and men may go, They will not break her heart, oh no Oh
POP.
-la! And men may come and men may go, They will not break her heart, oh no, Oh
CAS.
-la! And men may come and men may go, They will not break her heart, oh no, Oh
KHAD.
-la! And men may come and men may go, They will not break her heart, oh no, Oh
NOV.
-la! And men may come and men may go, They will not break her heart, oh no, Oh
CHO.
-la! And men may come and men may go, They will not break her heart, oh no, Oh
-la! And men may come and men may go, They will not break her heart, oh no, Oh
-la! And men may come and men may go, They will not break her heart, oh no, Oh
cresc.
ff
CURTAIN.
Ped.
Ped.
Ped.

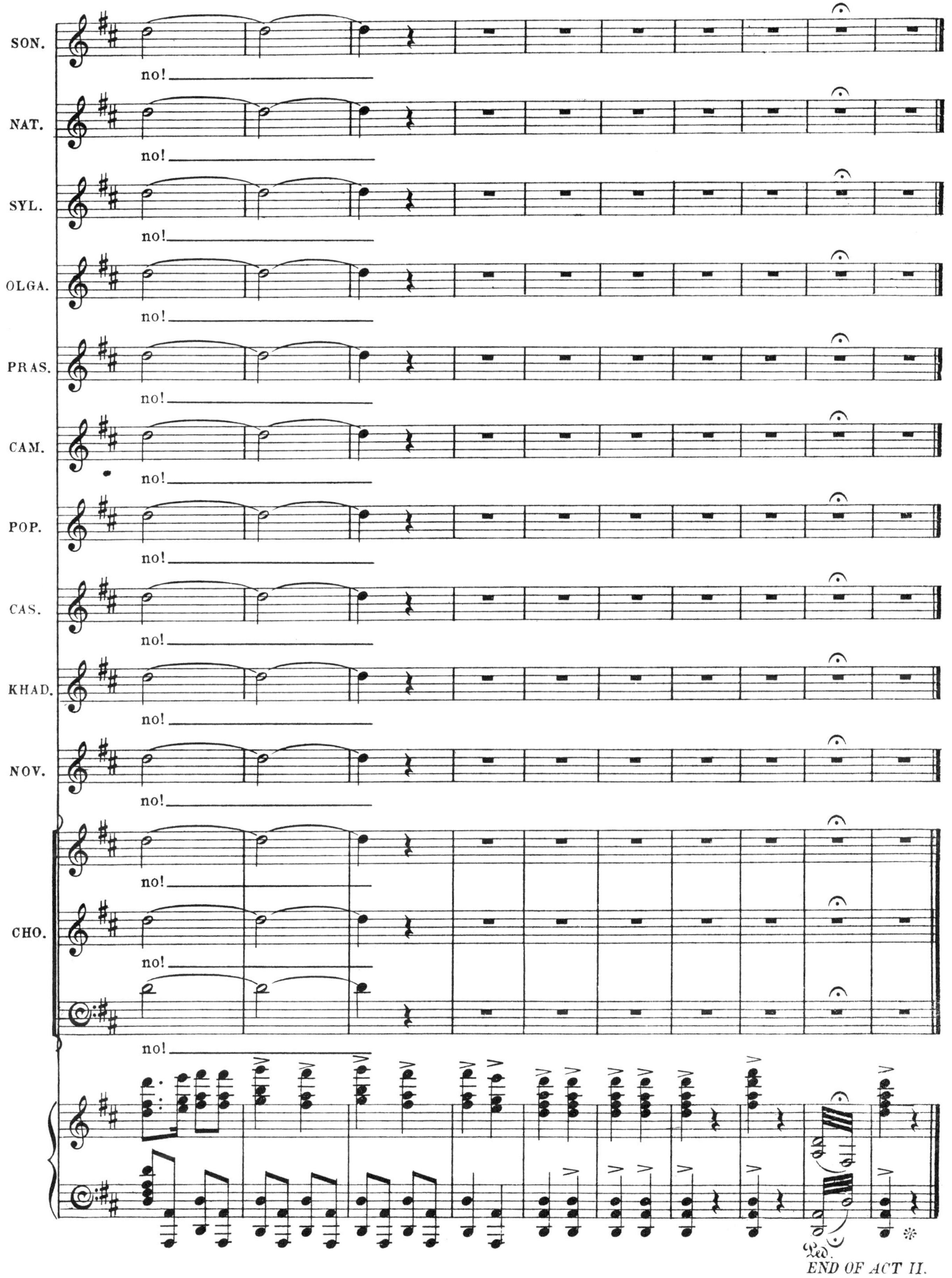
SON.
no!
NAT.
no!
SYL.
no!
OLGA.
no!
PRAS.
no!
CAM.
no!
POP.
no!
CAS.
no!
KHAD.
no!
NOV.
no!
no!
CHO.
no!
no!
Ped.
*

END OF ACT II.

Act III.

N° 13. OPENING SCENE.

No. 13a

CAKE-WALK.

fz
f
8va ad lib.
8va ad lib.
8va ad lib.
fz

No. 14. SONG. (Zozo) Six Girls and CHORUS.

"THE GIRLS AT MAXIM'S."

(Spoken.) And I!
ZO.
-lo! Do-do! Jou-jou! Frou-frou! Clo-clo! Mar-got!
ZO.
When a fit of blues at-tacks him. What should an-y fel-low do?
ZO.
Come and look for us chez Max-im, We are here to com-fort you.
ZO.
Tripping, tripping as we pass, Sipping, sipping in your glass, Tripping, sipping,
6. GIRLS.
Tripping, tripping as we pass, Sipping, sipping in your glass, Tripping, sipping,

ZO.
simply ripping, Come with us and take your lass. We can sing and tell you stories,
6. G.
simply ripping, Come with us and take your lass.
p
mf
ZO.
Pretty, witty, often true; We are Maxim's greatest glories, And we're here to
ZO.
welcome you. We're the little Paris ladies, That's the way a Maxim maid is. Lo_
6. GIRLS.
We're the little Paris ladies, That's the way a Maxim maid is.
f
p

ZO.
-lo Do-do! Jou-jou! Frou-frou! Clo-clo! Mar-got!
ZO.
Ri-tan-tou, ri-tan-ti-
6 GIRLS.
La, la, la, la, la, la, la, la, la, la, la, la, la, la!
ZO.
-relle. Eh, voi-là que je suis belle! Ri-tan-
ZO.
-tou, ri-tan-ti-ri, La plus belle de Pa

ZO.
ris! Ri-tan-tou, ri - tan - ti - relle, Eh, voi -
6 GIRLS.
Ri-tan-tou, ri - tan - ti - relle, Eh, voi -
f
f
Ped.
ZO.
- là que je suis belle! Ri-tan-tou, ri - tan - ti -
6 G.
- là que je suis belle! Ri-tan-tou, ri - tan - ti -
ZO.
- ri La plus belle de Pa - ris.
6 G.
- ri La plus belle de Pa - ris.
ff
Ped.

Marcia.
ZO.
Dance with us, if you are a-ble, Sing-ing, spring-ing to the tunes,
pp
ZO.
Or we'll dance up-on the ta-ble, In and out a-mong the spoons.
mf
ZO.
Sing-ing, spring-ing to the band! Swing-ing, cling-ing to your hand!
6 GIRLS.
pp
Sing-ing, spring-ing to the band! Swing-ing, cling-ing to your hand!
pp
ZO.
Spring-ing, fling-ing glass-es ring-ing, Just as long as we can stand!
6 G.
Spring-ing, fling-ing glass-es ring-ing, Just as long as we can stand!
p

O.
Here is mu - sic, here is danc - ing, Play - ing, sway - ing, all night through!
mf
We are Maxim's girls entranc - ing, And we're here to wel - come you! We're the
6 GIRLS.
We're the
f
lit - tle Pa - ris la - dies, Each of us a Max - im maid is! Lo -
6 G.
lit tle Pa - ris la - dies, Each of us a Max - im maid is!
p
(Spoken) And I!
- lo Do - do! Jou - jou! Frou - frou! Clo - clo! Mar - got!
f

Più Allegro.
ZO.
Ri - tan - tou, ri - tan - ti -
6 G.
La, la, la, la, la, la, la, la, la, la, la, la, la, la! Ri - tan - tou, ri - tan - ti -
Piu Allegro.
ZO.
- relle Eh, voi - là que je suis belle! Ri - tan -
6 G.
- relle Eh, voi - là que je suis belle! Ri - tan -
ZO.
- tou ri - tan - ti - ri La plus belle de Pa -
6 G.
- tou ri - tan - ti - ri La plus belle de Pa -

ZO.
-ris. Ri-tan-tou, ri - tan - ti - relle. Eh, voi-
6 G.
-ris. Ri-tan-tou, ri - tan - ti - relle. Eh, voi-
f
f
ZO.
-là que je suis belle! Ri - tan-tou, ri - tan - ti -
6 G.
-là que je suis belle! Ri - tan-tou, ri - tan - ti -
ZO.
-ri. La plus belle de Pa - ris!
6 G.
-ri. La plus belle de Pa - ris!
ff
Ped.
Ped.

Tempo di Galop.
ZOZO.
Ri - tan-tou, ri - tan - ti -
LOLO.
Ri - tan-tou, ri - tan - ti -
DODO.
Ri - tan-tou, ri - tan - ti -
JOU-JOU.
Ri - tan-tou, ri - tan - ti -
FROU-FROU.
Ri - tan-tou, ri - tan - ti -
CLO-CLO.
Ri - tan-tou, ri - tan - ti -
MARGOT.
Ri - tan-tou, ri - tan - ti -
NATALIE.
Ri - tan-tou, ri - tan - ti -
SYLVAINE.
Ri - tan-tou, ri - tan - ti -
OLGA.
Ri - tan-tou, ri - tan - ti -
CASCADA.
Ri - tan-tou, ri - tan - ti -
St. BRIOCHE.
Ri - tan-tou, ri - tan - ti -
CHO.
Ri - tan-tou, ri - tan - ti -
Ri - tan-tou, ri - tan - ti -
Ri - tan-tou, ri - tan - ti -
Tempo di Galop.

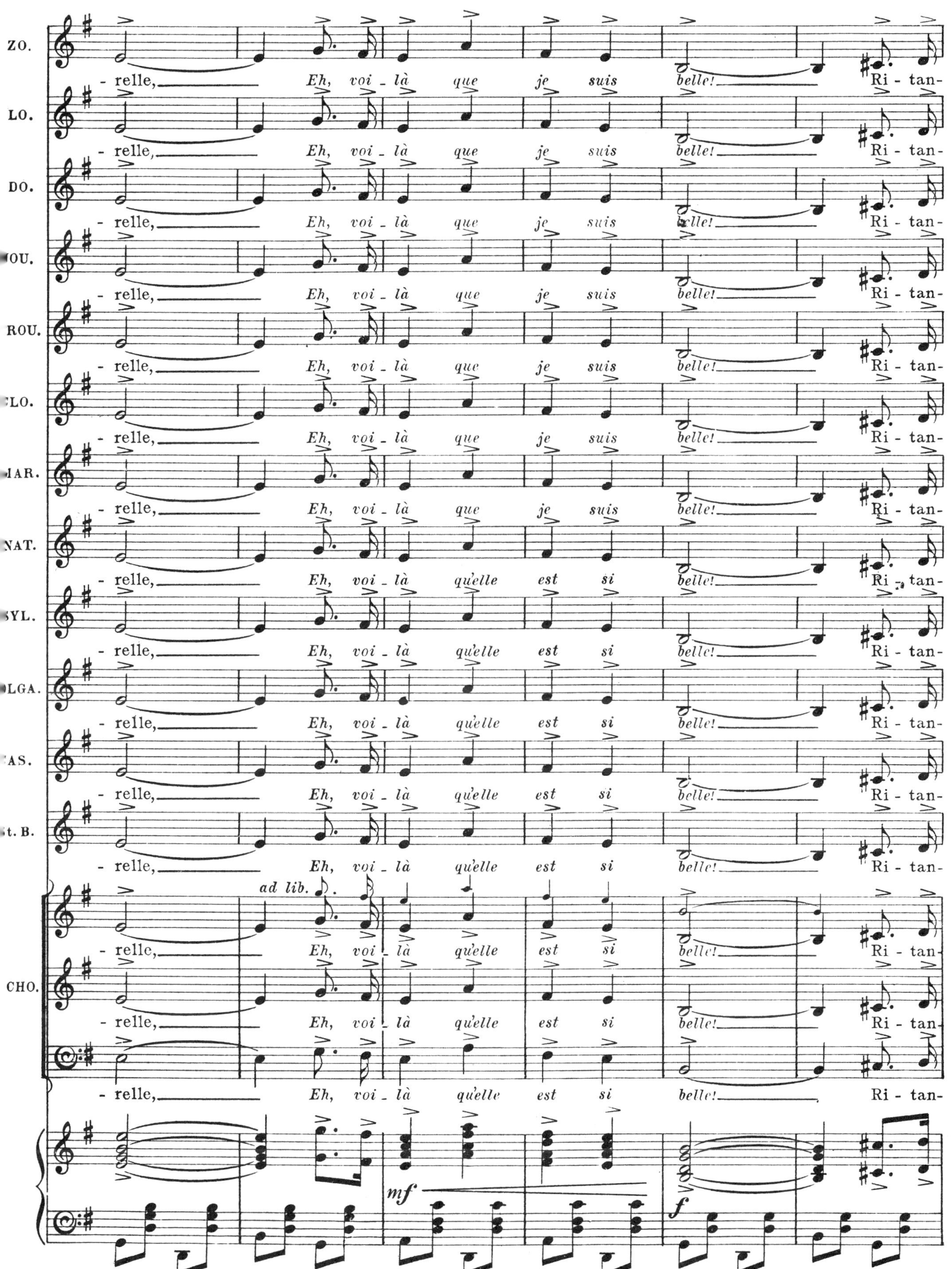
ZO.
-relle, Eh, voi-là que je suis belle! Ri-tan-
LO.
-relle, Eh, voi-là que je suis belle! Ri-tan-
DO.
-relle, Eh, voi-là que je suis belle! Ri-tan-
OU.
-relle, Eh, voi-là que je suis belle! Ri-tan-
ROU.
-relle, Eh, voi-là que je suis belle! Ri-tan-
LO.
-relle, Eh, voi-là que je suis belle! Ri-tan-
AR.
-relle, Eh, voi-là que je suis belle! Ri-tan-
NAT.
-relle, Eh, voi-là qu'elle est si belle! Ri-tan-
YL.
-relle, Eh, voi-là qu'elle est si belle! Ri-tan-
LGA.
-relle, Eh, voi-là qu'elle est si belle! Ri-tan-
AS.
-relle, Eh, voi-là qu'elle est si belle! Ri-tan-
t. B.
-relle, Eh, voi-là qu'elle est si belle! Ri-tan-
ad lib.
CHO.
-relle, Eh, voi-là qu'elle est si belle! Ri-tan-
-relle, Eh, voi-là qu'elle est si belle! Ri-tan-
-relle, Eh, voi-là qu'elle est si belle! Ri-tan-
mf
f

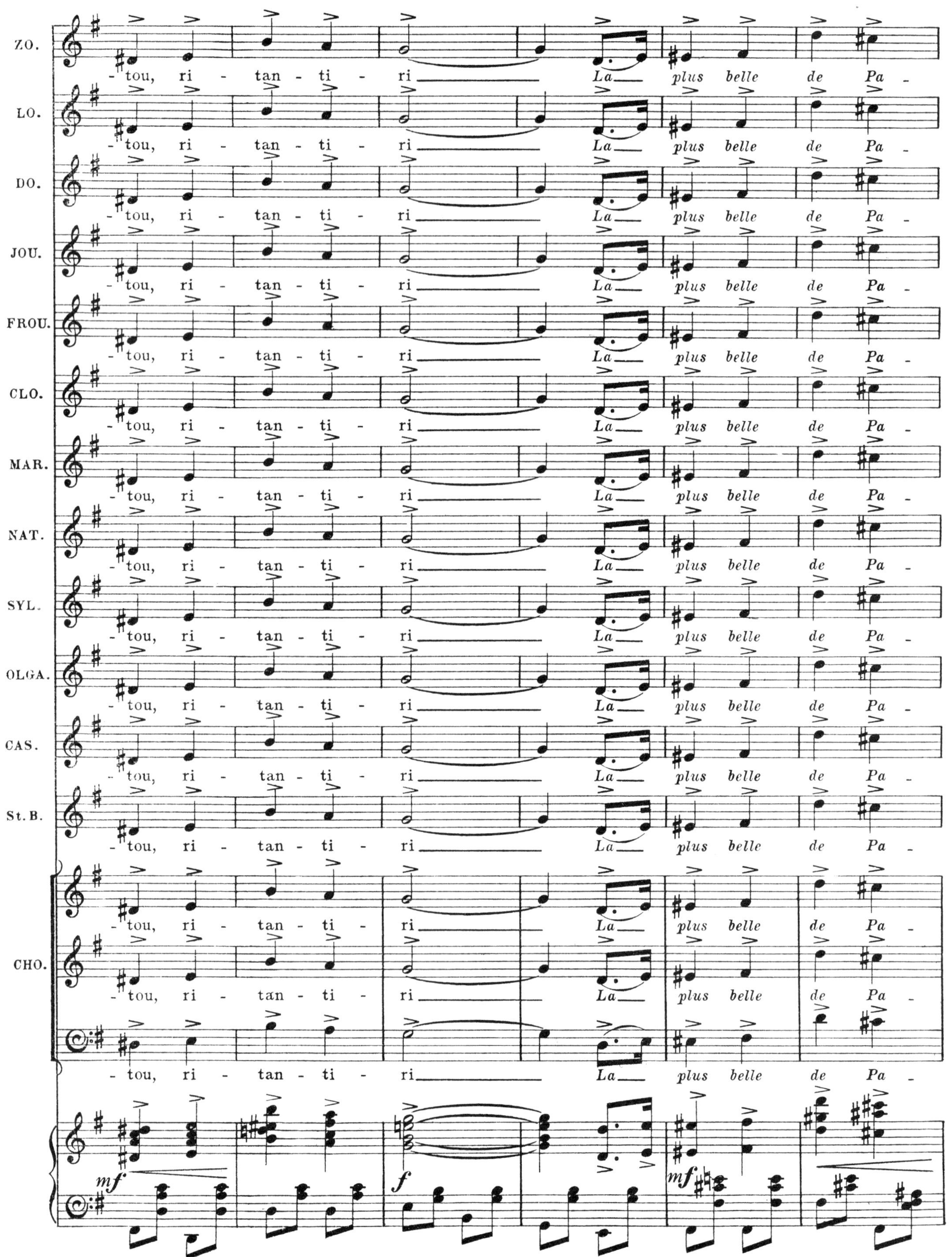
ZO.
-tou, ri - tan - ti - ri La plus belle de Pa -
LO.
-tou, ri - tan - ti - ri La plus belle de Pa -
DO.
-tou, ri - tan - ti - ri La plus belle de Pa -
JOU.
-tou, ri - tan - ti - ri La plus belle de Pa -
FROU.
-tou, ri - tan - ti - ri La plus belle de Pa -
CLO.
-tou, ri - tan - ti - ri La plus belle de Pa -
MAR.
-tou, ri - tan - ti - ri La plus belle de Pa -
NAT.
-tou, ri - tan - ti - ri La plus belle de Pa -
SYL.
-tou, ri - tan - ti - ri La plus belle de Pa -
OLGA.
-tou, ri - tan - ti - ri La plus belle de Pa -
CAS.
-tou, ri - tan - ti - ri La plus belle de Pa -
St. B.
-tou, ri - tan - ti - ri La plus belle de Pa -
CHO.
-tou, ri - tan - ti - ri La plus belle de Pa -
-tou, ri - tan - ti - ri La plus belle de Pa -
-tou, ri - tan - ti - ri La plus belle de Pa -
mf
f
mf

ZO.
LO.
DO.
JOU.
FROU.
CLO.
MAR.
NAT.
SYL.
OLGA.
CAS.
St. B.
CHO.
- ris! Ri - tan - tou, ri - tan - ti - relle. Eh, voi -
f
Ped.

ZO
la que je suis belle! Ri - tan - tou, ri - tan - ti -
LO.
là que je suis belle! Ri - tan - tou, ri - tan - ti -
DO.
là que je suis belle! Ri - tan - tou, ri - tan - ti -
JOU
la que je suis belle! Ri - tan - tou, ri - tan - ti -
FROU.
là que je suis belle! Ri - tan - tou, ri - tan - ti -
CLO.
là que je suis belle! Ri - tan - tou, ri - tan - ti -
MAR.
là que je suis belle! Ri - tan - tou, ri - tan - ti -
NAT.
là quelle est si belle! Ri - tan - tou, ri - tan - ti -
SYL.
là quelle est si belle! Ri - tan - tou, ri - tan - ti -
OLGA.
là quelle est si belle! Ri - tan - tou, ri - tan - ti -
CAS.
là quelle est si belle! Ri - tan - tou, ri - tan - ti -
St. B.
là quelle est si belle! Ri - tan - tou, ri - tan - ti -
CHO.
là quelle est si belle! Ri - tan - tou, ri - tan - ti -
là quelle est si belle! Ri - tan - tou, ri - tan - ti -
là quelle est si belle! Ri - tan - tou, ri - tan - ti -
sempre più prestissimo
Ped.
*

ZO.
LO.
DO.
JOU.
FROU.
CLO.
MAR.
NAT.
SYL.
OLGA.
CAS.
St. B.
CHO.
-ri La plus belle de Pa-ris!
ff
Ped.
Ped.

Nº 15.

DANCE.–(Fifi.) and CHORUS.

"BUTTERFLIES."

f

CHORUS IN UNISON.
CHO.
1. We are the dear lit - tle but - ter - flies that hov - er
2. Plen - ty of men try to cap - ture us and net us,
p 2nd f
All a - round a lov - er, And for beau - ty none can match us!
No - bo - dy can get us, We are ve - ry hard to cap - ture!
We flut - ter by you up - on a breeze of laugh - ter
Pray try a - gain and you will not al - ways miss us.
Won't you come af - ter Us and catch us!
If you should kiss us, Oh, what rap - ture!
1.
2.

DANCE.

accel:
poco a
poco al fine
f

Nº 16. SONG (Nisch.) and CHORUS.

"QUITE PARISIAN."

NIS.
now a great suc - cess In the way of mod - ern dress; From my
Pa - ris I can eat À la mode pe - tite mar - mite, And I
NIS.
Lon - don hat to my shi - ny toe, Quite Rue de Pim - li - co.
drink Cog - nac with that love - ly stuff Tarte à la pomme de truffe!
NIS.
That is the cut for me-
Give me su - prême de veau,
NIS.
Made in Pic - cad - dil - lee! For I am
Bœuf à la Chi - ca - go! For I am
rit.

REFRAIN.
IS.
quite Pa - - ri - si - - an, A most dis - tin - guished
quite Pa - - ri - si - - an, A most dis - tin - guished
man, And try to look as Eng - lish as I can. Yes, I'm a
man, I dote on sau - sage à la black and tan! Yes, I'm a
gay Pa - - ri - si - an, And far a - bove the
gay Pa - - ri - si - an, I get ten cour - ses
com - mon mob- Je suis très snob! For he is
for one bob- Je suis très snob! For he is
CHORUS. unison
f
f marcato

CHO.
quite Pa - ri - si - an, A most dis - tin - guished man, He
quite Pa - ri - si - an, A most dis - tin - guished man, He
CHO.
tries to look as Eng - lish as he can. Yes, he's a gay Pa -
dotes on sau - sage à la black and tan! Yes, he's a gay Pa -
CHO.
- ri - si - an, And far a - bove the com - mon mob, Il
- ri - si - an, He gets ten cour - ses for one bob- Il
CHO.
est très snob!
est très snob!
NISCH.
2. In my
3. In my
p

NIS.
Fa_ther_land a _ far Ve_ry nice the la_dies are, And the
NIS.
na_tive dan_ces are no_ble sport— Done in skirts that are un peu court. But the
NIS.
lit _ tle girls in France Are the ones I take to dance; They are
NIS.
all so chic and the der_nier cri Kick_ing up lin _ ger _ ie!

NIS.
Quite é - pa - tant; eh, what?
C'est jo - li - ment co - cotte! For I am
rit.
REFRAIN.
quite Pa - ri - si - an, A most dis - tin - guished
man, And an - y one can see I can can - can! Yes I'm a

NIS.
gay Pa - ri - si - an! They kick my top - per
NIS.
off my nob Je suis très snob!
CHORUS. (unison.)
f
For he is
f marcato
CHO.
quite Pa - ri - si - an, A most dis-tinguished man, And
CHO.
an - y - one can see he can can - can! Yes, he's a gay Pa -

CHO
-ri - si - an! They kick his top-per off his nob Il
CHO
est très snob!
Allegro.
DANCE.
p
ff
ffz

No. 16a

REMINISCENCE.

Lo-Lo, Do-Do, Jou-Jou, Clo-Clo, Frou-Frou, Margot and Danilo.

(*Interrupted by entrance of* SONIA.)

Nº 17. VALSE DUET.–(Sonia and Danilo.)

"I LOVE YOU SO"

DAN.
may not Let you hear, Yet the
sway - ing Dance is say - - ing, Love me, dear!
Ev - 'ry touch of fin - gers Tells me
what I know, Says for you, It's true, it's
Ped.
Ped.

DAN.
true, You love me so!
SONIA.
rit:
And to the mu_sic's
rit:
Valse lento.
SON.
chime, My heart is beat_ing time, As if to give a
Ped.
SON.
sign, That it would say, Be mine, be mine! Though our
pp
Ped.
SON.
lips may say no word, Yet in the heart a voice is heard. You can_not choose but
Ped.

SON.
know I love you so.
p animato
simile
SONIA.
allargando
Ev - 'ry touch of fin - gers
DANILO.
Ev - 'ry touch of fin - gers
allargando

SON.
tells me what I know. Says for
DAN.
tells me what I know. Says for
SON.
you, It's true, it's true You love me
DAN.
you, It's true, it's true You love me
Allegro.
SON.
so!
DAN.
so!
Allegro.
f
Ped.

Nº 18.

FINALE.–ACT III.

SON.
NATALIE.
LOLO, DODO, JOU-JOU.
FROU-FROU, CLO-CLO, MARGOT.
DANILO.
It is deep - er than
POP.
wo - man's too much for a man!
NOV.
Oh the women! Blow the women!
KHA.
Oh the women! Blow the women!
Oh the women! Blow the women!
CHO.
Oh the women! Blow the women!
Oh the women! Blow the women!

SON.
Girls, girls, girls, girls!
NAT.
Girls, girls, girls. girls!
LO.
DO.
JOU.
Girls, girls, girls, girls!
FROU.
CLO.
MAR.
Girls. girls, girls, girls!
DAN.
div - ing for pearls, Court-ing girls, girls, girls, girls, girls!
POP.
Girls, girls, girls, girls!
NOV.
Girls. girls, girls, girls!
KHA.
Girls, girls. girls. girls!
CHO.
Girls, girls. girls, girls!
Girls. girls. girls, girls!
Girls, girls, girls, girls!
f
ff

SON.
— With her fair flax-en hair, eyes of blue! — She's a long way too know-ing for
NAT.
— With her fair flax-en hair, eyes of blue! — She's a long way too know-ing for
LO.
DO.
JOU.
— With her fair flax-en hair, eyes of blue! — She's a long way too know-ing for
FROU.
CLO.
MAR.
— With her fair flax-en hair, eyes of blue! — She's a long way too know-ing for
DAN.
— With her fair flax-en hair, eyes of blue! — She's a long way too know-ing for
POP.
— With her fair flax-en hair, eyes of blue! — She's a long way too know-ing for
NOV.
— With her fair flax-en hair, eyes of blue! — She's a long way too know-ing for
KHA.
— With her fair flax-en hair, eyes of blue! — She's a long way too know-ing for
CHO.
— With her fair flax-en hair, eyes of blue! — She's a long way too know-ing for
— With her fair flax-en hair, eyes of blue! — She's a long way too know-ing for
— With her fair flax-en hair, eyes of blue! — She's a long way too know-ing for
f

SON.
you! She is dark, or she's fair, She may smile or may frown, Ne-ver
NAT.
you! She is dark, or she's fair, She may smile or may frown, Ne-ver
LO.
DO.
JOU.
you! She is dark, or she's fair, She may smile or may frown, Ne-ver
FROU.
CLO.
MAR.
you! She is dark, or she's fair, She may smile or may frown, Ne-ver
DAN.
you! She is dark, or she's fair, She may smile or may frown, Ne-ver
POP.
you! She is dark, or she's fair, She may smile or may frown, Ne-ver
NOV.
you! She is dark, or she's fair, She may smile or may frown, Ne-ver
KHA.
you! She is dark, or she's fair, She may smile or may frown, Ne-ver
you! She is dark, or she's fair, She may smile or may frown, Ne-ver
CHO.
you! She is dark, or she's fair, She may smile or may frown, Ne-ver
you! She is dark, or she's fair, She may smile or may frown, Ne-ver
ff
Ped.
*

Presto.

SON. mind, you will get done brown!

NAT. mind, you will get done brown!

LO. DO. JOU. mind, you will get done brown!

CLOU. CLO. MAR. mind, you will get done brown!

DAN. mind, you will get done brown!

POP. mind, you will get done brown!

NOV. mind, you will get done brown!

KHA. mind, you will get done brown!

CHO. mind, you will get done brown!

mind, you will get done brown!

mind, you will get done brown!

Presto.

ff

ff

Ped. * Ped. * Ped. *

END OF OPERA.